"Spiritual journeys are interesting things, and Todd's is one of the more interesting—from leader of the Vineyard churches, to house church pastor, to head of Alpha USA, and now an Anglican bishop. I've known Todd through many of these incarnations and we have not always agreed, but I have always been impressed with his passion for God and heart for others. In this book, you will find both—and my guess is that you will be challenged to think more deeply about your own spiritual walk. Todd reminds us that the church is not a place to go to, simply another meeting, but the way God has chosen to make himself known in our world."

ED STETZER, *president, LifeWay Research*

"As both a participant and leader, Todd has been at the heart of the evangelical world over the past thirty years. He has seen its strengths and weaknesses and at times has been profoundly disillusioned. But through it all he has never stopped loving the church. In *Giving Church Another Chance*, Todd is calling Christians to something better, something profoundly deeper and more exciting—a fresh vision of spiritual formation that is rooted in worship, life together and the kingdom of God. I think he has hit the nail on the head. After reading this book, you will never think about worship and spiritual practices the same way."

JIM BELCHER, *pastor, Redeemer Presbyterian Church, and author of* Deep Church

"If you have lost your way regarding church, Todd Hunter can show you the way back. His candor, theological nuance, grasp of history and willingness to name names (including his own) make this book unlike most you will read on this topic. Todd is one of the most Jesus-centric leaders speaking to the church today. Read this book to regain an appreciation for church as well as a deeper love for the One for whom the church exists."

JIM HENDERSON, *executive director,* Off the Map

"Most of those who criticize the church today have no idea what it is. Todd Hunter can help you find out, as he takes you along on his own pilgrimage of discovery—on the inside. The church is a unique stream of spiritual life— life 'from above'—flowing through a brief period of human history and into an eternal 'beyond.' Jesus Christ is the only one in charge of it, and we are the ones who today need a second chance. If you listen carefully to Hunter, you might begin to find The Church—perhaps without benefit of edifice, but then there too. If you do, your heart will sing with joy."

DALLAS WILLARD, *author of* The Divine Conspiracy

"Candid and evangelical, autobiographical and confessional, *Giving Church Another Chance* positions Christian practices right where they belong: at the life-shaping core of Christian life and Christian community."

PHYLLIS TICKLE, *author of* The Great Emergence *and* The Divine Hours

"With a self-revealing and down-to-earth style, the author asks readers to see all the church stuff—all the aspects of what happens in worship—as team exercises that get Christians ready for the real game in the world. *Giving Church Another Chance* is a challenging and refreshing invitation to understand again what Sunday morning is meant to be in the context of the whole week."

THE MOST REV'D ROBERT DUNCAN, *archbishop of the Anglican Church in North America*

"What you are holding should carry a government health warning: the reading of this book is good for your soul. But beware: it may cause you to fall in love with the church again, and the romance of 'repracticing' your faith may be habit-forming."

LEONARD SWEET, *author of* So Beautiful: Divine Design for Life and the Church

"I am thrilled about this book because in it, Todd is bringing hope to the church. It is a theological impossibility to not be part of the church if you are a follower of Jesus. Todd brings that reality into tangible ways of living as the church. It is easy to dismiss the church and think we can be okay on our own, but that is not what the Scriptures teach, nor is it healthy for us. We need the church and each other. This is a refreshing perspective on being church together."

DAN KIMBALL, *author of* They Like Jesus but Not the Church

Giving Church Another Chance

FINDING NEW MEANING

IN SPIRITUAL PRACTICES

TODD D. HUNTER

FOREWORD BY SCOT McKNIGHT

IVP Books

An imprint of InterVarsity Press
Downers Grove, Illinois

InterVarsity Press
P.O. Box 1400, Downers Grove, IL 60515-1426
World Wide Web: www.ivpress.com
E-mail: email@ivpress.com

InterVarsity Press® is the book-publishing division of InterVarsity Christian Fellowship/USA®, a
student movement active on campus at hundreds of universities, colleges and schools of nursing in
the United States of America, and a member movement of the International Fellowship of Evangelical
Students. For information about local and regional activities, write Public Relations Dept.,
InterVarsity Christian Fellowship/USA, 6400 Schroeder Rd., P.O. Box 7895, Madison, WI
53707-7895, or visit the IVCF website at <www.intervarsity.org>.

All Scripture quotations, unless otherwise indicated, are taken from The Message.
Copyright © 1993, 1994, 1995, 1996, 2000, 2001, 2002. Used by permission of NavPress Publishing
Group. All rights reserved.

Design: Cindy Kiple
Images: burning match: Thorsten Rust/iStockphoto
       smoke: iStockphoto
       burning candle: ensiferum/iStockphoto

ISBN 978-0-8308-3748-9

Printed in the United States of America ∞

Library of Congress Cataloging-in-Publication Data

Hunter, Todd D., 1956-
  Giving church another chance: finding new meaning in spiritual
practices / Todd Hunter.
       p. cm.
  Includes bibliographical references.
  ISBN 978-0-8308-3748-9 (cloth: alk. paper)
  1. Spiritual life—Christianity. I. Title.
BV4501.3.H859 2010
248—dc22

                                                              2009042068

P 22 21 20 19 18 17 16 15 14 13 12 11 10 9 8 7 6 5 4 3 2 1

Y 28 27 26 25 24 23 22 21 20 19 18 17 16 15 14 13 12 11 10

For Richard Foster, Dallas Willard and Eugene Peterson.

Teachers and leaders in the Way of Jesus,
they never gave up on the spiritual practices of church.

We walk in the light of their wisdom and humility.

Contents

Foreword

We've turned two corners.

The first corner is that the deconstructive phase of criticizing the church (or churches or denomination or the institutional church or The Church) as a sport is behind us. We've moved on. Increasingly I'm seeing numbers of emerging Christians who—while they know the deconstructive phase was important for them for getting back to Jesus and to the core of the Christian faith—know that the church is where God is at work, and an increasing number who want to make the church better. The age of innocence is also behind us, but we know that somehow God's work in the church is not finished and we are called to participate in what God's mission for the world is. Instead of casting the church as perfect and then pointing out how far short it falls, an increasing number of Christians recognize their own failures and that the problem is "me" and "us" and not the church.

The second corner is individualism. Modernity, the story goes, ratcheted the human self up and then put the individual at the center of the story. Somehow, and sometimes in good but occasionally naive ways, that individualism has reshaped how the Christian faith is understood. A number of my friends describe what has happened to the church as consumerism—Christians go to church to "get" something and when they don't, they find a church where they can get what they want. Sometimes the spiritual formation movement itself has been infected by this same individualism and consumerism: we pray, we practice solitude, we fast and we meditate *in order to aggrandize our spiritual condition.* There is a better way.

Todd Hunter, in the book in your hands, gracefully embodies getting beyond deconstruction and getting beyond individualism or consumerism. If deconstruction criticized the church, Todd illustrates the beauty of Christ's body. If individualism makes the church an option and spiritual disciplines something designed only for the individual's growth and churches a place where we go to get something, Todd shows that *what the local church routinely and orderly performs each week can reshape who we are and empower churches to embody the gospel.* In this book, routines will take on new meaning.

What this book does is something I've longed for: instead of casting all of spiritual disciplines as something we do as individuals, Todd suggests in this book that there are "ecclesial," or church-shaped or group-shaped, disciplines that are gifts from God for the church. A passage that came to mind over and over as I read this book comes from Paul, in Ephesians 2, and it describes the fellowship where God's Spirit is at work as discussed in this book:

> Consequently, you are no longer foreigners and strangers, but fellow citizens with God's people and members of God's household, built on the foundation of the apostles and prophets, with Christ Jesus himself as the chief cor-

nerstone. In him the whole building is joined together and rises to become a holy temple in the Lord. And in him you too are being built together to become a dwelling in which God lives by his Spirit. (vv. 19-22 NIV)

"We" are that dwelling, together, but we are only that dwelling because "we" are in Christ and because God's Spirit dwells among "us."

Scot McKnight
Karl A. Olsson Professor in Religious Studies
North Park University

Preface

From Churched to Dechurched to Rechurched

"[Practices] are essential to finding our way.
Practices are not for know-it-alls. Practices are for those
who feel the need for change, growth, development, learning.
Practices are for disciples."

BRIAN MCLAREN

This book is written for everyone who has tried church and found it wanting, but somewhere deep within they still desire a spiritual life in the way of Jesus. I understand; it happened to me.

In 1991, after twenty-five years of walking with Jesus, I found myself struggling to connect church to the practices of my daily life. For the first time in my life I was not excited about going to church. My faith in Jesus and his kingdom agenda was strong. But the activity of church was troubling me.

MY CHURCH ROOTS

I grew up in a stereotypical 1960s Southern California–style, liberal United Methodist Church. I was raised in a godly community of laypeople who were sincerely following the New Testament's *one anothers* (love, serve and be patient with one another, etc.). But we were surrounded by leaders who followed the latest ideas coming from progressive Christian thinkers.

While I did not hear much of the gospel, as I would come to know it, I do have fond memories of my preschool to high school days. I remember my mom's best friends. It was a multigenerational church, and some of Mom's friends were her age; others were old enough to be her parents. I have a profound recollection of the sense of community that pervaded the congregation. Thus my childhood was theologically plain—nothing stuck to me—but it was relationally warm. Most of today's talk about community within emerging church circles would have been old hat to the loving, pious 1960s people I grew up with.

In 1976, I was a nineteen-year-old college freshman who for years had withstood the evangelistic efforts of the Jesus People, but I finally "gave my life to Christ" or "got saved" through the ministry of Greg Laurie of Calvary Chapel, Riverside, California—now Harvest Christian Fellowship. I absolutely loved Calvary Chapel. So much, in fact, that some pride filled my heart about how I had moved on from the *errant* Methodists!

At Calvary my spirituality was infused with Jesus, the Bible and evangelism. In hindsight I think of my time at various Calvary Chapels as a form of contemporary fundamentalism. I mean this mostly in a good way. Some of the "end times" stuff was a little over the top, but we managed to hold on to and convey the basics of the Bible in relevant ways. Now thirty-some years later, when people are having a hard time believing anything at all, my Calvary years seem wonderfully innocent.

While attending Calvary Chapel Bible School I met John Wimber, then the pastor of Calvary Chapel, Yorba Linda. Later John, along with Kenn Gulliksen, became the founder of The Vineyard churches. I was in my early twenties when I met John and did a church planting internship with him in 1978–1979. He and I and our families became lifelong friends. When John joined with Kenn to start the Vineyard movement, out of personal loyalty, not a beef with Calvary, I went with them. Eventually, in 1994, I became the national coordinator and soon thereafter the president of Vineyard Churches USA.

Looking back on my time with the Vineyard, I am hugely and sincerely grateful to have learned from John the gospel of the kingdom of God, an interactive life with the Spirit, worship and leadership. But again hubris was in my soul, and an attitude of *We're cool, you're not; we're doing it right, you're not* filled my sinful heart.

DISCOVERING THE NEED FOR NEW PRACTICES

For the first ten years of its existence the Vineyard operated with a set of values I admired and to which I wholeheartedly agreed. We said we were going to be normal regarding the work of the Spirit. We were going to be "naturally supernatural," not taking on airs of religiosity, superiority and the like. We were going to be humble and simple. We vowed to never manipulate anyone, but to always affirm the dignity of all persons. We committed to never exaggerating the work of God and to other beautiful values too numerous to name here.

John and Carol Wimber, in my recollection, naturally brought these attitudes to the work of the Spirit from their Quaker (John and Carol) and Catholic (Carol) heritage. I loved it. Those values gave me permission to seek the person and work of the Holy Spirit without getting nutty. They removed the fear of going overboard in ways that would harm ourselves or others. These solidly ethical values released faith and the freedom to take risks.

Ten years or so after the founding of the Vineyard, while serving as John's right-hand man in the Vineyard Anaheim, new values and practices came to us from outside groups. At this time I shut down out of confusion and fear. This is the part where I bear the most blame. I tried, at times, to sound the alarm, but in truth I also chickened out. I'd be in rooms with people who were household names at that time and think, *So-and-so is smarter than me. She prays more. That guy has God appear to him regularly. He is my boss*, and so on.

Over time my mixed behavior—sometimes speaking up, other times shutting up—led to a loss of my own sense of personhood. I liked neither the transformation of the Vineyard nor the person I was becoming. For the twelve years prior to this, my ministry life was marked by joy and adventure. Sure, there were hard times, but they were not of our own making, like this was. For me the main problems were not the public issues we faced but the behind-the-scenes realities. As a result, I had a crisis of confidence in the church. I hold no grudges against any of the principals involved. Many good things happened in that era—that is part of what made it so darn confusing!

I left my role in the Vineyard Anaheim to move to Virginia Beach, Virginia, to minister in a Vineyard there. But that was just the surface reason. Truth be told—and I told it at the time—I *needed* to get out of town! I needed to get "on my own" again, like a young adult leaving home. I don't know how I knew this, but deep inside I recognized that I needed to find a way to take responsibility for my part in and my reactions to what had happened in the Vineyard Anaheim.

Thus when I arrived in Virginia Beach I immediately enrolled in seminary. My thought was that, had I known just a little church history, a little more theology, I could have been more present, more self-differentiated and more confident in those Vineyard meetings. I also began some counseling to process why I was having such a hard time "standing up straight on the inside," as I explained to my counselor on our first visit.

As great as those two processes were, the most powerful things began to happen in me when, in an effort to reengage some basic Christian practices, I picked up Richard Foster's *Celebration of Discipline*. From Richard I discovered Dallas Willard, Eugene Peterson and many other ancient and contemporary writers who educate and train others on the practices associated with Christian faith.

During this time, I began to read the early editions of *The Message*, and this passage became particularly meaningful:

> So Paul took his stand in the open space at the Areopagus and laid it out for them. . . . Starting from scratch, [God] made the entire human race, . . . with plenty of time and space for living so we could seek after God, and not just grope around in the dark but actually *find* him. He doesn't play hide-and-seek with us. He's not remote; he's *near*. We live and move in him. . . . The unknown is now known,

and he's calling for a radical life-change. (Acts 17:22, 26-28, 30)

Meditating frequently on this portion of Scripture, I came to love the visual impression I had of Paul *taking his stand*. I knew I needed to find a way to take my stand as well. I came to value the notion that we had plenty of space to seek after God. For me this *space* represented the grace and patience of God, along with me not having to be perfect, being able to slow down and not be driven by my neurotic need to accomplish things. I was captured by the idea that God was calling for a radical life change. I knew I wanted just that, but I was only beginning to see where it might come from.

THE EMERGING CHURCH

Recapping the timeline here, I was in Virginia Beach from 1991 to 1994. In 1994, I moved back to Anaheim to be the national coordinator—and later president—of Vineyard Churches USA. As 1998 rolled around I was doing better with self-differentiation but continued to struggle to find a confident way of practicing church. By 2001 I had left my role with the Vineyard, and on a professional level (pastor, teacher, mentor) I focused on researching the nature of the church. My family tried all kinds of things: local churches of various kinds, house churches, home meetings that were not formal house churches.

Seeing the early signs of millions of people struggling with church, I began to experiment with what was called "alternative" or "emerging" forms of church. My motive was to find ways of doing church that made sense to postmodern, post-Christian America.

While the values of dialogue, community and creativity

within the emerging church movement are valid, and while I have huge sympathy for what the emerging church is trying to do, I found their theology getting too fuzzy and their evangelism drying up. I also found that new expressions of church can inadvertently exploit religious consumerism on par with the best and biggest "vendors of religious goods and services" out there! With little to no evangelism happening, and still battling consumerism, I became increasingly puzzled and anxious, maybe even a little depressed over church.

I was getting desperate to find a way to do church that actually enabled life in the kingdom of God as taught by Jesus. I was looking for a church that was less mechanistic, less driven by numbers, less hierarchical and less weird. In two different places—Orange County, California, and Eagle, Idaho—I worked with groups of mostly young people who were hurt and turned off by church. These friends were barely hanging on to God. To some degree we were able to correct the things that were bothering us about church, but we managed to create our own problems that were just as bad or worse than what we left! I take responsibility for this. I was the leader, after all, looking for the right trail to follow, but I kept running into frustrating boulders along every path.

A POSITIVE HOLISM

Each of these places where I met God in the past—the United Methodist Church, Calvary Chapel, the Vineyard, emerging churches and my present home in the Anglican Church—have become the seedbed for a new way to approach the spiritual practices of church. I am seeking to bring the best of all of them—Word, Spirit, liturgy (with calendar and offices), and spiritual disciplines—to bear on this new work.

I did not intend any of this history. Neither did I approach any of it with premeditation. It just unfolded before me. And I feel in no way victimized by it. I have no complaints, I hold no grudges, and there are no chips—at least that I can see—on my shoulder. At this point in my life, I essentially have positive memories and appreciation for everything each tradition and each group gave me. The message here is *not* that everything and everyone in my past was wrong, and now I have found the right church: the Anglican Church. I know better.

The real message is that finding a way to repractice faith of any denominational brand is mostly about each of us. The focus here is on our ability to engage with the spiritual practices of church for the purpose of our own spiritual transformation first, with being Christ's ambassador for the sake of others a close second.

I am a better person today because of all the people and events of those various eras of my life. As I look back, all the pros and cons of my life were simply opportunities to learn to walk with God as a leader for the sake of others. I blew it a lot. I only tell the story to give the context from which my need to repractice church surfaced. You need to know my background and biases so we can do good work together in this book. While I am sincere in writing, you need to be alert to any bias I blindly hold. As Rob Bell likes to say, "God has spoken; everything else is commentary—right?"

During the period I did not regularly attend church, I realized that a big ingredient in my search for a repracticed faith does not come from things external to me, like eras of my life, segments of the church or denominations, but things internal to me—slices of my heart, portions of my soul. Somehow, though, during my "dark night of the church," I realized that I could not simply stay away from church. Staying away, I found, had no constructive power. What I needed was an affirmative way to reengage *the spiritual practices of church*. Come with me, and I'll show you what I mean.

Acknowledgments

Any book rooted in real life is collaborative effort. This one is no different.

Beginning with my family, I'd like to acknowledge those who were most helpful in shaping my writing. My wife, Debbie, has been along with me for the ride of "repracticing church" the whole time. Listening to her honest struggles and her more recent liturgical enlightenments has significantly shaped my thoughts and convictions.

My children, Jonathan and Carol, have not been able to avoid the twists and turns of their parents' journey. While I'm sure they have their own ups and downs related to our family story, they at least have had an open and honest view of the church. Conversations with Mom and Dad have always been as open as they wanted—no holds barred—no question too naive, no statement too hostile.

I also need to thank the earliest members of my new church plant, my faith community—Holy Trinity Anglican Church in Costa Mesa, California. All of us are both excited and committed to the notion of practicing our corporate, liturgical faith such that it facilitates spiritual transformation and propels us into a missional engagement with others we connect with in the rhythms and routines of our actual, existing lives—in the various places we have organic community: work, neighborhood and play.

I would like to recognize the Anglican Mission in America—especially Archbishop Emmanuel Kolini, who provides oversight, and Bishop Chuck Murphy, Anglican Mission chairman—as they have shown great trust in me. I hope the decade ahead will confirm that confidence. I am appreciative of all my new colleagues in the Mission who have been amazingly patient with my zillions of questions about all things liturgical.

I am grateful for my agent, Kathy Helmers, who helped shepherd into being my first two books with InterVarsity Press.

Speaking of InterVarsity, my editor, Cindy Bunch, is a hero of mine. She mixes solid intellect, editorial expertise and warm friendship in the most wonderful ways. I am a nervous author, but Cindy always manages to get me through the process with her patience and my little faith intact. Her colleagues at InterVarsity Press share her servant-hearted traits too. I thank you all.

Special thanks also to J. I. Packer for two solid days of training in Anglican history and theology. Jim does not deserve blame for my less-mature reflections, but any helpful thoughts in this book are a credit to his tutoring.

I can never think back on the last ten years without being indebted to all the young leaders across America who have let me hear their innermost thoughts regarding church and how, or whether, it could work in our current culture. As these capable and bright women and men unwrapped their hopes and fears, their visions and doubts, I received an education that flows into the writing of this book. Thank you, my dear friends!

Reflecting on these young leaders brings to mind one of their most cherished teachers: Scot McKnight. Scot's wide influence far outdistances his main teaching role. Scot has been a theological and practical leader among young ministers and among his colleagues, like me. Thanks, Scot, for a thoughtful foreword.

Finally, chief acknowledgment goes to Richard Foster, Dallas Willard, Eugene Peterson and their lovely wives. Many times over the past decade, in moments of genuine despair about church, I would close my eyes and picture each of these modern leaders of the Christian faith, hand-in-hand with their spouses, humbly walking into relatively unknown churches, greeting their friends, settling in for worship and engaging in the practices of church. My next thought after thinking of these couples was always: *If these mentors of mine, my leaders in the follower-ship of Jesus, are making church a priority, maybe we younger, pessimistic upstarts have something to learn from them.* Their faithfulness to practicing church according to their various traditions—Quaker, Vineyard, Baptist, Presbyterian, whatever—has put me on the path to rediscovering new meaning in the spiritual practice of church.

Introduction

Doing the Faith for the Sake of Others

Sitting around the living room having coffee and cold drinks
with Christian friends, the conversation turned to a favorite
topic: church bashing. Almost all criticisms of church—"All I
do is look at the back of other people's heads"; "The music is
out of date"; "The preaching is boring"; "The pastors are selfish and manipulative"; "The staff is clueless or hypocritical"—
assume that *church* means what happens on Sunday morning.
Think about it: when have you ever heard criticisms of how
the dispersed church practices its faith—except when there is
a major moral scandal of a famous Christian? It seems to me
that 98 percent of church criticism has to do with one hour of
the weekend.

What if we could shift from seeing church as *doing our weekend duty* to seeing the historic elements of church as spiritual
practices—as a springboard for a way, an order, a practice or a
structure for spiritual life? Lighting a path to that springboard
is the burden of this book.

Jesus always envisioned and communicated an embodied real-life and put-into-practice version of Christianity. He was into the *game*, not the pregame meetings. Only recently has mere belief in a few points of doctrine concerning Jesus—rather than playing his game—meant that a person is a Christian. For Jesus, merely hearing and agreeing with his teaching was never enough; nor was it enough to be awed by his miracles. His teachings and actions are signs that point to the reality we are invited to *live*. Did you catch that? *Live*, not just "believe true" or "feel warm about," like memories of a favorite Thanksgiving Day.

The following words of Jesus, spoken at the end of his most famous teaching, make this abundantly clear:

> These words I speak to you are not incidental additions to your life, homeowner improvements to your standard of living. They are foundational words, words to build a life on. If you work these words into your life, you are like a smart carpenter who built his house on solid rock. Rain poured down, the river flooded, a tornado hit—but nothing moved that house. It was fixed to the rock.
>
> But if you just use my words in Bible studies and don't work them into your life, you are like a stupid carpenter who built his house on the sandy beach. When a storm rolled in and the waves came up, it collapsed like a house of cards. (Matthew 7:24-27)

Jesus' life, words and work illumine and bring to bear the kingdom of God on earth. They create on earth the reality humans are intended to live in—an interactive, cooperative friendship with God. As an overflow of that relationship we become ambassadors of that in-breaking reality. When things go right, ambassadorship happens in natural, unforced and uncoerced ways. Given a choice between building on rock or sand, builders always prefer rock. No one would think this choice extreme, out of the norm or "over the top." For us to build on the Rock, we must put what we learn in church and Bible reading into practice. Though we sometimes think such obedience is over the top, it is the rock on which the good life, the truly and fully human life, is built.

But why has "just using Jesus' words in Bible study" predominated? What is the history behind this pattern? One reading of Christian history suggests that it arose in an attempt to assure Christians of salvation, which was supposed to be accomplished through believing a set of minimal Christian doctrines. Providing mental and emotional certainty is commendable. During the Reformation, the liberation of uneducated, mostly illiterate people from the unethical manipulations of the church through a minimum set of beliefs was an honorable goal.

Doing this required focusing on Bible study. And in some cases this motivated people to put Jesus' words into practice. But in our day, much like the unintended consequences of subprime mortgages and the deregulation of banking, Bible study for assurance of salvation has come with some very expensive hidden costs.

One interesting and subversive way to get at this is to think about what Christians don't normally argue about. We tend not to argue about *how* to be patient or kind. When was the last time you heard of a debate between Christian leaders over the proper *way* to love someone who is hurting us? There aren't schools of thought regarding kindness. These questions arise only among those seeking to *practice* what they read. Looking for ways to intelligently put Jesus' words into practice is the blueprint for building life on the rock, for Christian growth.

CHRISTIAN PRACTICES DO NOT
ARISE OUT OF THE BLUE

When we moved to Virginia Beach in 1991, it was the year some aircraft carriers were returning from the first Gulf War. It was awesome to see formations of fighter jets in the sky. Sometimes as many as sixteen jets would circle the base as one by one they broke formation and landed at Oceana Naval Air Station. I loved scanning the sky for fighter jets.

I remember one incident in particular. Driving home from work one afternoon, I was heading east toward the beach when out of nowhere, seemingly just a few feet above the pine trees, an F-14 came roaring into view. For a second I thought it might fly right through the windshield! I can still feel the chill as that jet leaped into view out of the blue sky.

The spiritual practices of church are *not* like that. They do not suddenly appear out of the blue. They arise within a context, an ongoing story wherein God has actually had an interactive relationship with his people. In fact the same is true about the F-14. Though it appeared *out of the blue* to me, it too was flying within a context, probably a training flight related to the larger story of defending our nation.

In our day the spiritual practices associated with church seem to appear *out of the blue*. In this context "out of the blue" means something like having no practical value or being from another world or time that has no bearing on contemporary life; they are disconnected from reality. But I want to show you that the kind

30

of genuine Christian spirituality you've been dreaming of is possible by repracticing the spiritual routines of church.

WHAT IS *REPRACTICING*?

What do I mean by *re*practicing? I am highlighting the traditional observances usually associated with church life. Because many of these practices are currently held in low esteem, this will seem counterintuitive at first. But hang in there with me and you'll discover some powerful pathways to following Jesus in faith through the basic practices of the church.

Let me give you one example of refreshing a spiritual activity by "repracticing" it. Millions of people have tried to observe a *quiet time*, getting up at 4:30 or 5:00 a.m. to pray, read a chapter of the Bible or fill in the blanks of their current Bible study. But it left their actual life, the rest of their day, untouched. Practiced like that, quiet time often just made people tired and irritable—the very thing they might have been trying to change! These sincere people then remained hungry for something more real, more authentic and more connected to the actual routines of their life. They need to "repractice" quiet time.

We need a fresh vision of spiritual formation, one that puts the church and traditional Christian observances in their proper place. I want to create a new vision and stimulate our imagination about Christian practices. I want to show that God created the church and its associated practices not as an end but the means to an end. As we move along, I will explain the role the spiritual practices of church have in the kingdom and how they are empowered by the Holy Spirit. I will demonstrate their place in the wider purposes of God, in culture and in the formation of the followers of Jesus.

HISTORIC CHRISTIAN PRACTICES AS
A SPRINGBOARD TO LIFE

Not many of us have convincing models for actually doing what Jesus said. There are not enough examples in the recent history of the church to shape our imagination this way. Within many of us there is a strong push-pull, approach-avoidance tussle concerning the spiritual practices of church. I know I am afraid of getting it wrong, going overboard or not going far enough. I have found that for many of us our first thought about seriously practicing the words and model of Jesus is *this could go wrong.* Where then do we find help? Are there some beginning steps, some training wheels or rails to run on?

It may sound odd to say, but a good place to start is with the historic practices of the church. Unfortunately, some of these practices have become rote or even meaningless. But in the hands of sincere followers of Jesus they have a genuine, sustaining power for life in the kingdom of God. They have facilitated spiritual formation and service to others for a couple thousand years.

Thus when I embarked on a search to find ways to make the habits of Christianity and church significant and valuable, I used the *old* as a launching pad for the repracticed *new.* This is not to disparage the old. We don't watch a space shuttle launch and walk away disparaging the launch pad. Rather we are blown away—maybe literally!—by its ability to put something into orbit. Similarly, I use the historic practices of Christianity as a launching pad to propel me into fresh ways and means, practices, to pursue spiritual transformation.

THE PROPHET SENGE

I'll never forget it. At the time, I'd never seen anything like it. Highly regarded thinker and author Peter Senge was due to speak at a very large conference. I was there to learn and to play a minor teaching role. This was a unique meeting for Christian leaders who were trying to think about the future of the church. For a reason I cannot remember, Senge could not get to the venue in the Denver area. At the last moment the conveners of the conference arranged to have him appear via a satellite feed from his home. As I sat there in the vast auditorium with a couple thousand others, I realized we were like hungry little birds looking for whatever crumbs he would drop into our nest.

This was almost a decade ago. Satellite hookups at church conferences were not as common as today, so there was some buzz in the room. Even more uncommon, it was a little risky in those days to have someone who practices and advocates Zen meditation speak to a large group of evangelical leaders. Soon though, fulfilling our hopes, Senge showed up: an enormous face on one of the biggest screens I had ever seen.

I'm sure Senge talked for an hour on a number of topics. But for nine years I've had one quote rattling around in my head:

> I'd also like to argue that the mainstream of Christianity throughout the last fifteen hundred years, and particularly evident in the last two hundred years, has been for the majority of practitioners not a practice-oriented religion but a Sunday religion, a religion of "do what you want as long as you subscribe to the right things and you show up on Sunday to keep the institution going.

"Brother and sisters," an old-school preacher might say at this point, "this should not be!" Though I conceptually agree with the old-school reaction, my motive is not to scold. My purpose is to describe and inspire. To describe the life available to us through Jesus in the kingdom of God and to persuade, inspire and encourage you to pursue it through reconceiving the spiritual practices of church.

There is a unique hunger in the Western world for a practiced, embodied religion. This is so for at least two reasons. First, people are increasingly skeptical of religion that only affects the mind of its adherents (and then their supposed eternal destiny). It seems intuitively wrong to the average person today that a person can claim to believe in Jesus, maybe even believing that he died and rose again, but live badly at work, in the neighborhood and at home.

Only a few misguided, often angry people expect Christians to be perfect. But the Christian cry "we can't be perfect" has become an excuse that has simultaneously stymied the spiritual growth of churchgoers and turned off the onlooking world. It has become a subconscious way to avoid intentionally living in alignment with Jesus' words, a rallying cry that allows us the take on Jesus' words as "incidental additions to your life, homeowner improvements to your standard of living" rather than "foundational words, words to build a life on" (Matthew 7:24-25). The words of Jesus are subconsciously seen as mere words used in Bible studies, not to be worked into our life.

CHOOSING FAITH OVER CYNICISM

For many of us, picking up spiritual practices means leaving behind attitudes that immobilize us like bugs on sticky paper.

Some seekers are sincerely stuck by pluralism and relativism. There can be no movement until we make a choice, a commitment to following Jesus and the things he said. But this can be emotionally and mentally uncomfortable. Society is quickly moving to the notion that religion is the enemy of social progress. Believing in or discussing the uniqueness of Jesus is now, in many circles, a serious social sin.

No matter what the present day, socially correct, postmodern vibe says, we must entrust ourselves to something, to decide to follow one path and not others. Commitment *is* possible, even necessary. As the apostle Paul said, we don't have to grope around in the dark forever (Acts 17:22-32). But to follow Jesus, we need to bind ourselves to him and his message of the kingdom of God. (But this doesn't mean we cannot learn from others, even the best of other religions when they align with God and his story.)

I have heartfelt empathy with those seekers who are legitimately stymied by the problems they see with truth. Context is a real issue. Perspective and the power and limits of language can play a confusing part too. But the problems associated with context, perspective and language do not add up to the idea that there is no truth and that nothing is real. This is not the place for a long discussion on truth, but there are a couple things we should think about. First, the modern world has made truth's domain too small, that is, only that which can be proved by science. The postmodern viewpoint has opened up many other possibilities. Seeing those possibilities and admitting their validity is appropriate. But the postmodern view tends to keep us from making choices, especially when we know that our choice is colored by our context, perspective and

cultural conversation. Choosing, of course, is of utmost importance for following Jesus. No one slips up and suddenly finds he
or she is following Jesus. We *decide* to follow him.

Belief (or faith) is not having a good time of it right now. In
some circles, certain pet doctrines or beliefs are hammered on
and held as if they are the whole of Christian faith. In other
circles, belief and faith are passionately shunned as the relics of
times past. Worse they are sometimes sources of division, even
hate. To recover their rightful place in Christian life, beliefs
need to be *actualized*, that is, we turn them into practices that
(1) change us for the better in a way that (2) those around us
experience as for their own good.

FROM BELIEFS TO PRACTICES

In mid-December 2008 I did a Google search for "Christian beliefs" and "Christian practices." There were 636,000 listings for
practices and 1,080,000 for beliefs. Do we care about beliefs approximately twice as much as we care about practices? Does this
imbalance seem to fit the person, work and message of Jesus?

The goal of repracticing Christianity is to move our spiritual
experience from a mere system of beliefs and unsatisfying
church routines to a newly conceived *way of life* and empowered living rooted in the spiritual practices of church. The goal
isn't to become more "religious," as that term is negatively used
today. The goal is "life, life and more life," and alignment with
God's creation intention for humanity. We seek this because we
believe what Jesus said:

Anyone here who believes what I am saying right now and
aligns himself with the Father, who has in fact put me in
charge, has at this very moment the real, lasting life and is

no longer condemned to be an outsider. This person has taken a giant step from the world of the dead to the world of the living. (John 5:24)

Almost everyone I know thinks that if authentic spirituality, the real and lasting life of which Jesus speaks, could be identified, they would seek it immediately.

Bishop and scholar N. T. Wright helps us see how this works in conjunction with renewed spiritual practices of church. No one I know paints a better portrait of what it might look like for our generation to practice faith in the real world.

When the church is seen to move straight from worship of the God we see in Jesus to making a difference and effecting much-needed change in the real world; when it becomes clear that the people who feast at Jesus' table are the ones in the forefront of the work to eliminate hunger and famine; when people realize that those who pray for the Spirit to work in and through them are the people who seem to have extra resources of love and patience in caring for those whose lives are damaged, bruised, and shamed, then it is not only natural to speak of Jesus himself and to encourage others to worship him for themselves and find out what belonging to his family is all about, but it is also natural for people, however irreligious they may think of themselves as being, to recognize that something is going on that they want to be part of.

THE FRAME OF REFERENCE

The basic assumptions, then, that undergird what follows in this book are:

- The church and its associated practices are presently held in low esteem.

- Millions of reasonable and sincere people believe the church is incapable of producing the spiritual life they are seeking.

- The blame for this state of affairs does not belong solely to the activities associated with church but also to our inability to connect with the church's spiritual practices, which serve as a launching pad for life, outside of church, in the way of Jesus.

In the chapters that follow I will show you how the spiritual practices of the church can become the first steps on the path to life—real and lasting life in Jesus.

1

Going to Church

Being Sent as Ambassadors of the Kingdom

"The method of the kingdom will match the message of kingdom. The kingdom will come as the church, energized by the Spirit, goes out into the world vulnerable, suffering, praising, praying, misunderstood, misjudged, vindicated, celebrating: always as Paul puts it in one of his letters— bearing in the body the dying of Jesus so that the life of Jesus may also be displayed."

N. T. WRIGHT

I played serious baseball while in college—well, serious to me! I was a catcher. Before every game we had meetings for pitchers and catchers to go over scouting reports and how we would pitch every batter. We discussed which opposing hitters were hot at the time, which players were not hitting certain pitches in certain parts of the strike zone, and where batters tended to hit certain pitches so we could position the defense. As important as these meetings were, we never mistook them for the *game*.

Those meetings prepared us for the real thing: the competition. Church and its historic activities and practices should be viewed in the same pregame manner. They enable us to do what we long to do: excel as followers of Jesus in the 167 hours per week we are not in church.

This is not a perfect analogy, but to help you see how the spiritual practices of church work with being *sent* by Christ, think of athletics and other public performers. Those of us who have watched a major athletic event or professional performance on television have probably seen an athlete in a locker room or performer in a dressing room engaged in deep, personal, private time. Perhaps they are visualizing and imagining just how they want to sing on stage or attack their opponent on the field. Maybe they are quietly filling their minds with positive thoughts, remembering the times they have done well, believing that they can do so again. These are common practices of elite performers.

Now imagine you left the TV but have come back an hour later and the event is running late. The camera crew is looking for the performer, who is still in the dressing room, in *church* mode. That would be odd. No performer ever confuses the preshow preparation with the show. The former always exists for the latter. It leads to the stage.

Most every human activity has meetings associated with it. Corporate marketing teams meet, sports teams meet, surgical teams meet, teachers meet—but none of them confuse the meetings with the real task. Meetings exist to facilitate the actual work.

As fed up as many people are with church meetings, I don't think the church needs to quit meeting; nor does it need to make the meetings more hip. The people of God have met weekly in tabernacles, temples, church buildings and homes for thousands of years, and they will continue to do so. But the church needs to rethink the purpose of its meetings.

ACCEPTING THE CHURCH FOR WHAT IT IS

I am not *antichurch*, and this book is not a critique of the church. I assume that church is what it is, for better or for worse. This book is about the spiritual practices of the church as a launching pad to life. Like most human endeavors, the church has meetings associated with it. Unfortunately, while most people do not confuse meetings with their work (the game or show), churchgoers often do.

I have discovered that Christianity is not just composed of the right stuff, accurate beliefs and correct ingredients. Over the years I learned that I needed to find some right *practices* to make the right stuff work. A rocket can be assembled with all the right parts, but if someone messes up launch procedures, the whole thing turns into a catastrophe. Lots of people, from various disciplines and points of view are wondering aloud today whether the church has become a catastrophe of sorts.

In response to my own experience, and taking into consideration the critics of Christianity, I believe we have discovered all the right bits of stuff, assembled them and defended them from the contrary elements of society, but we forgot *how* to launch the rocket.

I believe in "going" to church. I go every week. I have been a church leader since I was nineteen years old. But I have also experienced a five-year hiatus from normal Sunday meetings. (Don't worry, I didn't "forsake meeting together" with the body of Christ; I just experimented with other forms of church.) At first it felt good to be liberated.

But it wasn't so great, actually. I found that in my "anti-church" home or coffee shop groups and many of the others I have known, the focus stays on the meeting: what style, who leads, when and where we meet and so forth. Thus I dare say that we need to repractice church—no matter time, location, size, leadership—so that the natural fruit becomes followers of Jesus who are ambassadors of God's kingdom

A REPRESENTATIVE AND REPRESENTING PEOPLE

In 2 Corinthians 5:19-21 Paul implies that corporate *ambassadorship* is a loose synonym for *church*.

> God was reconciling the world to himself in Christ, not counting men's sins against them. And he has committed to us the message of reconciliation. We are therefore Christ's *ambassadors*, as though God were making his appeal through us. We implore you on Christ's behalf: Be reconciled to God. God made him who had no sin to be sin for us, so that in him we might become the righteousness of God. (NIV, emphasis added)

For us, these two things are not usually synonymous. Church is one thing—someplace we go for worship, teaching and fellowship—and being an ambassador is another. *Worship, learn* and *fellowship* are not the first words you associate with an ambassador. An ambassador is someone with *position*, delegated *power* and the duty to *act* or *represent*. How can these terms linked in Paul's mind be so divergent in ours? Because, we have sawn in two what was intended as a whole.

The term translated "ambassador" is customarily used to connote someone who is a trusted elder; an envoy who travels as an authorized agent or representative on behalf of another. Interestingly, Paul says that in the new way of Jesus, in the Spirit-empowered, Spirit-authorized church, God is trusting Jesus' people to be his envoys of the kingdom of God. Ambassadors are focused on the affairs of their own country (the will, agenda and story of God) as they reside in another country (their actual lives) they have been sent to. As ambassadors of Christ, we focus on the agenda of the kingdom of heaven, which is the rule, reign or action of God. We ambassadors are alert to the agenda of God in the places we live, work and play.

I can hear someone thinking, *I don't experience church as a launching pad for ambassadorship within the rhythms and routines of my life!* Maybe this is a good place for a confession: it is no secret that while pursuing religion it is possible to become something other than the shining example we envision when first heading down that path. Along the way lies the ditch of smugness, the pothole of judgmentalism, the rut of superiority and the crater of self-righteousness. Any pastor, spiritual director or counselor can tell you that connection to a church can expand or shrivel life. In fact, respected Christian author Philip Yancey says that he has been "in a life-long process of separating church from God."

We don't have to be particularly sympathetic to the church to recognize that this is an unfortunate state of affairs. How could the church become crosswise to the purposes of God? Perhaps the church itself is not so much the problem. I've been a pastor for decades, so I know that some churches are boring and out of touch, and that others are much more approachable and in tune with the times. If our critique ended here, the solution would be pretty easy—just get every church to be culturally cool! And that's not such a huge job. Stuffy boards, vestries and presbyteries notwithstanding, it is not so hard to culturally remodel a church. It surely is not like putting a man on Mars.

Unfortunately, something much more profound is going on, something way beyond how cool church is. Millions of Americans are also leaving cool churches in search of something more meaningful. The issue is not so much the contemporary nature of the church but its connection to God's purpose for the church. If we are to be living within God's story, and if God's story can be likened to a map, a narrative or a piece of music, then we should be asking, What map are we on? What narrative are we living in? or What music are we playing? These questions will lead us to see that church is mainly what happens outside of its meetings.

Many today say, "I'm spiritual, but not religious." But most of them are confused about what spirituality is. Here is the best definition I have heard: "Union in action with the Triune God is Christian spirituality."

All along the continuum of conservative to liberal, Christian groups have struggled with being genuine apprentices of Jesus. Most of our problems come from picking and choosing our favorite markers of discipleship and then purposefully or inadvertently ignoring others. I know this is oversimplified, but conservatives have often chosen Bible facts and witnessing, and liberals have chosen various social-justice issues.

These things are fine. It's just that there is so much more.

Not more *to do* or becoming more *religiously busy*, but more holistic, more at rest and peace as was Jesus our Master and Guide. In view here is a way of life marked by the kind of love found in 1 Corinthian 13, the kind of character exemplified in Galatians 5 and the *righteousness, peace* and *joy* of the kingdom Paul describes in Romans 14.

This fuller life works as we go out the front door, get off the subway, walk to the soup line, seek a parking space or hurry to church. The bottom line: apprenticeship to Jesus directs our whole life—not just the activities chosen from various right- or left-wing traditions.

There is a subtle but huge difference between Christianity viewed as something to *do* versus something to *live*. The word *do* implies rules, regulations and sheer obedience. *Live*, on the other hand, calls to mind holism, groundedness and thoughtfulness. *Lived* implies organic rhythms and routines. Eugene Peterson powerfully connects *believe, do* and *live:*

> No matter how right we are in what we believe about God, no matter how accurately we phrase our belief or how magnificently and persuasively we preach or write or declare it, if love does not shape the way we speak and act, we falsify the creed, we confess a lie. Believing without loving is what gives religion a bad name. Believing without loving destroys lives, believing without loving turns the best of creeds into a weapon of oppression.

It is true that Christians are commanded to do certain things. But in so doing *we* never "become the subject of the Christian life, nor do we perform the action of the Christian life. What we are invited or commanded into is what I call the prepositional-participation . . . of *with*, *in* and *for*." That is to say, God is always the subject, and God also performs the essential, difference-making action. We get in on it through the prepositions: we are *with* God, *in* God, *for* God.

YOU DON'T HAVE TO BE PERFECT

Showing others how to relate to God and his purposes for humanity is what Jesus was aiming for through his life and ministry. Though they are important, Jesus rarely talked about right beliefs. He never asked people to formulate proper theories regarding Noah, the flood or the ark. He didn't call people to an accurate hypothesis of why God called Abraham or how it was that Abraham and Sarah had a child. Jesus spoke about his obedience to his Father's will and invited others into his kind of life.

At this point you may be, figuratively speaking, wiping your brow while exhaling a big *Whew, I don't have to believe everything just right!* While we may need a deserved break regarding believing perfectly, it is no easier to behave correctly—to obey God in the way Jesus did—than it is to believe correctly. Both take a massive injection of God's grace and some simple cooperation on our part.

I know many of us have read the Great Commission a thousand times, but I'll bet very few of us have caught the highlighted bits below on the first couple hundred readings:

> Meanwhile, the eleven disciples were on their way to Galilee, headed for the mountain Jesus had set for their reunion. The moment they saw him they worshiped him. *Some, though, held back, not sure about worship, about risking themselves totally.*
>
> *Jesus, undeterred, went right ahead and gave his charge:*

"God authorized and commanded me to commission you: Go out and *train everyone you meet,* far and near, *in this way of life,* marking them by baptism in the threefold name: Father, Son, and Holy Spirit. Then *instruct them in the practice of all I have commanded you.* I'll be with you as you do this, day after day after day, right up to the end of the age." (Matthew 28:16-20, emphasis added)

Imagine that. Among his first ambassadors, Jesus identified some who held back, who were not sure about worshiping him—wondering whether worship were a whole-life thing, if it meant placing their life before God as an offering (Romans 12:1-2), whether it would cause them to risk themselves totally. But this did not deter Jesus. How in blue blazes does that work—that Jesus entrusts his whole agenda to a mixed group of people? Well, I think I know. When I go to church, I always find a mixed group of people, some holding back, some cruising along and others going for it full-throttle. Church members have not changed much in the last two thousand years!

Jesus commissioned his first followers with a special and unique task: to *train* others, to *instruct* them in Jesus' *practices,* in his *way of life. Train* sounds like a corporate term or the activities at a police or fire academy. *Pray* sounds like church or monastery. But to Jesus they are two aspects of learning *a way of life.*

CONFIDENCE FOR GOING TO CHURCH

This past year I had the joy of reading and endorsing a book for someone I have known for thirty years. Mark Foreman was my first teacher at Calvary Chapel Bible School in Twin Peaks, California. In Mark's book *Wholly Jesus* he writes what I consider to be one of the most holistic and unprejudiced observations and explanations of the church I have read in years. More than that, Mark's views on the church impart hope in a time when the church's reputation is very low. Mark gives us great help in moving from simply attending church to being ambassadors of the kingdom:

> My experience tells me that buildings are not the problem. Believers all over the world desire worship/training centers that allow them to move more quickly to advance the kingdom. Unbelievers as well are attracted to centers of worship. There is something very human about wanting a gathering place to worship.

Note the emphasis here is *to advance the kingdom*. That is precisely what ambassadors of the kingdom do—they represent, advocate for and advance the will of the one they represent. Jesus is our main model of an ambassador, of representing one kingdom to others. When pressed about what he was doing and why, sounding just like an ambassador Jesus routinely said something like "I only do and say what I hear and see my Father doing" (e.g., John 5:19-20).

Foreman also notes that all people have found themselves drawn to the spaces and places dedicated to worshiping God. Through all times and in all places, humans have met in every conceivable kind of building, edifice or structure for worship. And when they sincerely worship God, others are attracted.

God, it seems to me, is not interested, foremost, in our *buildings* and *styles*, and their power to attract outsiders. Rather, out of his self-revealing love and grace, God seems to be willing to meet with anyone at anytime, anywhere. I know of home churches that are about as low church as possible which are full of the glory of God! But I also know Catholic, Anglican and Orthodox communities—*high* churches—that are full of the life of God. The same can be said for everything in between: from Vineyard churches or nondenominational churches meeting in industrial parks to independent megachurches in the suburbs, all can spill over with the life of God. God doesn't seem to care about these things. He graciously grants his presence to all who call on him with sincere faith.

AMBASSADORSHIP: A MODEL FOR THE
PURPOSE IN PURPOSE-DRIVEN CHURCHES

Church, it seems to me, for all the angst it is producing, boils down to our imagination. Questions like Why does the church exist? or What are churches for? precede the question In what manner does the church exist? Rick Warren, knowing this better than most, gave us his famous *Purpose Driven Church*, sounding an alarm and guiding, teaching and equipping Christian leaders to create purpose-driven communities of faith. The community of faith in the book of Acts "viewed themselves as a transformational kingdom force inward to their [church] community and outward to the world."

On the other hand, many of my boomer contemporaries and I have been guilty of *playing business* with church. Foreman comments:

> We have everything reversed. We treat the church like a country club, a restaurant or a theater. We not only focus on the form, we are absorbed in it. Like neighborhood boys building a tree house, church planters tinker obsessively over creating the perfect form complete with the

best bylaws, philosophy, bulletin and logo. Once birthed, this obsession with form becomes the DNA of the church—the church members maintain the focus and invite others to come and see the form. I know of a church with a well-defined form that still has no mission to the world 30 years after the successive church plant.

I read these words and think, *Ya, those big-box churches . . .* But Mark is no such fool. He says, correctly in my view, that "house churches can be just as guilty—most believe their form is the right form. But the house church movement is a form reacting to another form. *In reality, there is no right form, only a right function—a right mission.*" This is an appropriate time to make a note in the margin or to put this book down and make some notes elsewhere—that's what I did when I first read that emphasized sentence. Mark taught me this thirty years ago, and it has now shaped my imagination for the church I am presently starting. Putting wheels to that ideal, Mark sums things up: "Church size, polity, style and building must follow function. Every facet of the ministry must have an outward component."

To repractice church in terms of ambassadorship we have to make sure the church does not eat up all our time or become our main focus. We are not trying to get people to follow a certain *form* of church but are trying to help them follow Jesus for the sake of others. The goal of leadership and the goal of our churches is that people discover the spiritual practices of church as a way of learning to follow Jesus.

CHURCHES AS EMBASSIES

What exactly does an ambassador do? To what kinds of activities is this metaphorical language pointing? Do God's ambassadors merely carry messages, just talk? Or do they *reveal* the message—the gospel? If the latter, it requires a whole lot more than talking. It suggests representing the whole good news of the in-breaking kingdom, not just talking about the gospel as if it were something merely for the ears. Rather, the gospel is for our whole life. The gospel is about God bringing to bear his complete will for all his creation—especially those counted as the least among us, those we think of last and those left out.

If, as I've suggested, an ambassador serves as the representative of a sovereign to another country, then the primary function of Christ's ambassadors is to bring God's whole message (the gospel of the inaugurated kingdom) to all creation. This is good news for both seekers and the frustrated members of church. It used to be that seekers and Christians were relegated to passive roles in the church. Now however, neither seekers nor Christians are willing to so reduce their faith quest. Both faith and growth these days are best facilitated by whole-life involvement.

Here is a key for church leaders: we should think in terms of reshaping our church communities into *embassies*, places where all can experience God through his ambassadors. Church becomes a serving, healing, welcoming, grace-filled interaction with God's representatives on earth. Then, as we scatter across the city, the spirit of that embassy goes with us, so that we are the emissaries of God when gathered *and* when scattered.

Something about this seems right to people today. And we should rejoice in this new intuition. I believe it is the work of the Holy Spirit. A participatory model has always been closer to our scriptural story than mere mental belief. The notion of ambassador is powerful because it is both biblical and contemporary. *Ambassador* suggests a meaningful role, not the raw power that is under so much suspicion today. Further, it imparts a vision for dialogue, community, relationship and interaction between groups of people. And the context is the contested, curious and sometimes noisy realities of the kingdom of God and the kingdoms of earth. *Ambassadors of the kingdom* have the power to heal several contemporary illnesses: the hunt for personal meaning, the quest for a place to belong and the longing search to matter to others.

KINGDOM AMBASSADORS:
A BASIC MODEL FOR FOLLOWING JESUS

While doing my internship with John Wimber I learned that the Lord's work is *humble caring*. He introduced me to Mother Teresa, noting her servanthood, her gospel of deeds and her single-hearted devotion to Jesus and the poor. John always gave us humble jobs to do. I did not know it until later, but he was checking our attitudes in case there was some spiritual formation we needed. Teaching us how to move from "churchy" work to being ambassadors of the kingdom, Wimber says, "We learn how to be servants of the master by imitating the way our master serves his Lord. Jesus did the Father's bidding on earth, the Father's will is all he did. . . . [H]e lived a life of total dedication to the service of God."

I am aware of a comprehension that has been growing in me over the past eighteen years. It started with discovering the spiritual formation literature I described in the preface. It continued as I wrestled with those ideas in concert with a growing understanding of the kingdom of God.

Next came an introduction to the Gospel and Our Culture

Network and the literature of the new missiologists who were way ahead of me in trying to put a kingdom emphasis and spiritual formation together for a missional church. They helped me see that church is best considered and conceptualized after we have done our proper theology—our thinking about the God revealed in the Bible. From there we can develop a theory and model of mission. So it works like this: theology (e.g., Christology, pneumatology and eschatology) gives meaning and shape to mission; once mission is clear we can ask, How do we do church that is true to and reflective of the person and mission of God?

FROM CHURCH TO AMBASSADORS: FROM INSTITUTION TO INCARNATION

Jesus' vision for his people is expressed in the Gospel of Matthew:

> You're here to be light, bringing out the God-colors in the world. God is not a secret to be kept. We're going public with this, as public as a city on a hill. If I make you light-bearers, you don't think I'm going to hide you under a bucket, do you? I'm putting you on a light stand. Now that I've put you there on a hilltop, on a light stand—shine! Keep open house; be generous with your lives. By opening up to others, you'll prompt people to open up with God, this generous Father in heaven. (Matthew 5:14-16)

My wife, Debbie, would never say she is a prime example of an ambassador, but she does not realize how well she makes the spiritual practices of church doable. Debbie keeps an open house and is generous with her life about as well as anyone I know! As an example, look at this snippet from a MySpace profile written by a friend of our daughter. When she uses the word *us* she means our daughter Carol and their group of friends from high school and the teen center where Debbie was a volunteer.

> [Carol's] mom is a complete sweet heart and will do anything for anyone. She takes me in, she makes me food, she pays for things, she drives us around and the most important, she loves and cares for us without asking anything but respect in return. I call her "mom" because she makes me happy; she cares for me and loves me as her own. She is beyond generous and I can't believe some of the things she does for me and the way she makes me feel. . . . These three Hunters have to be one of the highlights of my life. They literally keep me standing and make me strive for good without even knowing it.

Jen is a self-described agnostic. And while we've known this, it hasn't mattered at all in terms of our relationship with her. We genuinely love her (actually, both our children's friends) in the way Jen describes. Our son, Jonathan, is now twenty-four, but I know many of his friends would say very similar things about Debbie.

I don't tell this story to "puff" my wife, but as a clear and concrete illustration of *doable* mission. Debbie understands the connection Jesus talks about in Matthew 5. She knows that opening herself in love and generosity to others is a powerful door opener to faith. I don't know how many steps Jen has taken toward faith in the years we have known her. But Jen knows we are Christians and that we live as consistently Christian lives as we can.

The key point is that Debbie's life of doable mission is to Jen as powerful as any evangelistic crusade, tract, television or radio show could ever be. And this isn't just my opinion. Jesus said it first—I am simply following him: "Now that I've put you there on a hilltop, on a light stand—shine! Keep open house; be generous with your lives. By opening up to others, you'll prompt people to open up with God, this generous Father in heaven" (Matthew 5:14-16).

I hope with all my heart that Carol's and Jonathan's friends will indeed open up to God and find their generous Father in heaven. But I have never heard Debbie say that she does what she does for the friends of our children to manipulate or coerce faith in them. I doubt the thought has even crossed her mind. She is simply expressing the love God has given her— the light he has placed in her. And it has the effect Jesus said it would.

BEING A SENT ONE IS DOABLE

I wanted you to hear Debbie's story so you might believe the natural, organic mission is doable. In fact, today I would say it is more doable than ever. Why? Because, as someone has said, small is the new big! Reflecting on a famous quote by Mother Teresa, my friend Steve Sjogren often says that "small things done with great love can change the world."

We ought to think of the church as being similar to batting cages; art, dance or music studios; or language-acquisition programs. These help us practice something in order to do *the practiced thing* (hitting the ball, creating art or speaking the language, etc.) better in another environment. This is exactly what I did in the early years of my walk with Jesus. More recently I have seen that it is possible to embrace the church, warts and all, in healthy ways by engaging in its spiritual practices to train ourselves to be the worshiping friends of God—a people whose worship moves us to join God in his healing and rescue of everyone and all the earth.

Quiet Prelude

A Life of Centered Peace

"The endless pursuit of pleasure is leaving us numb."

SUBTITLE OF ARCHIBALD HART'S
THRILLED TO DEATH

I love walking up a set of steps of a certain old church building in town and passing through a narthex to find my seat about ten minutes early for church. I love those quiet moments of reflection with peaceful prelude music playing in the background. After getting the prayer book, hymnal and service bulletin situated, I survey the attractive ceiling, gaze at the beautiful stained-glass windows, take in the congregation of mostly white-haired people and mutter almost silent prayers. I'm always a little embarrassed to do this—afraid that I might be seen as less than cool for being in such a place by the folks from one of the large and loud churches in town. Maybe it is just me and perhaps it has to do with my extremely full life, but I crave the quiet, thoughtful moments the prelude music provides.

Lately I've been trying to figure out how to take that feeling with me so that the people in my life experience *me* the way I experience preludes. I've been thinking about how to live in the "peace be with you" (John 20:21 NIV) and peace that causes you to "not let your hearts be troubled" (John 14:1 NIV), the peace which "overcomes the world" (1 John 5:4 NIV) that Jesus promised, and the "righteousness, peace and joy" in the kingdom that Paul speaks of (Romans 14:17 NIV).

Maybe the prelude of a traditional worship service stands out to me because of my Methodist upbringing. The organ prelude conveyed to me, as a youngster, that we should quiet ourselves in preparation for worship—that worship was about to begin.

SEEKING PEACE

After twenty-four years of being a pastor, I found myself without a church to lead. I was still leading Christian organizations and helping others start churches, but I didn't have a church I was responsible for. During these years no one in my family was clamoring to go to church. We still were very much followers of Jesus, still committed to tithing and helping others, still committed to our growth in Christ. But somehow in the midst of all that, church as we had known it lost most of its appeal. We did go sometimes, and we have always been in a home group.

During this time, probably because of some internal wiring peculiar to me, I would occasionally feel the need to go to church. Surprisingly, when this urge would hit me, I would not feel drawn to the Vineyard—the main church my adult life—I was drawn to the Episcopal church downtown. This is curious because I am really fond of the Vineyard pastor in my town. We have known each other for more than twenty years. It is a really good church. On the other hand, I'd guess that the Episcopal church I occasionally visited is significantly more theologically liberal than me. And like most evangelicals of my generation, theology is very important to me.

So why couldn't I completely cut myself off from church? And why did I feel drawn to an Episcopal church? As I reflect on these intermittent visits, three things stand out: the gentle, reflective, centered, peaceful and focused feel created by the interior architecture; the preludes, prayers and creeds; and the Eucharist.

CONNECTING PRELUDES TO LIFE

What is a prelude? It is an introductory performance, action or event preceding and preparing for the principal or more important matter to come; it is preliminary. As we begin to explore the experience of preludes for the sake of living in settled peace, it is important to set aside a possible misunderstanding. I am not saying that quietly reflecting in the context of great architecture with lovely music playing in the background is the zenith of religious experience or the goal we all should aspire to. On the contrary I am saying that preludes are a means to a different kind of life, the life God intended for humanity.

Eugene Peterson is characteristically helpful on this topic: "Spirituality is not immaterial as opposed to material; not interior as opposed to exterior; not invisible as opposed to visible. Quite the contrary; spirituality has much to do with the material, the external, and the visible. What it properly conveys is living as opposed to dead." Like sipping a tasty, ice-cold bottle of premium root beer, let's drink a little more deeply at the well of Peterson's insightful words.

When I describe myself sitting in church settings, I don't mean to say that God is more present in a beautiful sanctuary and less so in my daily work world. Presence here is a matter of a different level of my conscious awareness of God, which is facilitated by sacramental means, sacrament being a visible sign of an invisible reality.

Second, though I described an inward reaction I have during preludes, I don't think this means that *inward* is superior to *outward* in creation and in the plan of God. Both are equally real—and God is equally present everywhere. But those two realities do *not* mean we should never do anything special to make ourselves more consciously aware of God. I value preludes precisely for the reason Peterson suggests: I am trying to connect the experience of preludes to an overcoming-spiritual-death kind of *life:* my goodness as a husband and father, my driving habits, the way I lead and supervise others, and so on. Peterson says it well:

> The end of all Christian belief and obedience, witness and teaching, marriage and family, leisure and work life, preaching and pastoral work is the *living* of everything we know about God.
>
> If we are going to *live* as intended, which is, to the glory of God, we cannot do it abstractly or in general. We have to do it under the particularizing conditions in which God works, namely, time and place, here and now.

Using preludes as a catalyst for living all the particulars of our lives through centered peace is the vision of this chapter.

To get there we must now turn our attention to the contemporary archenemy of our peace—the frenetic pursuit of excitement and pleasure.

THRILLED TO DEATH

Is it even feasible to think that we could find settled peace in our manic, broken and up-to-the-minute bad-news world? In the summer of 2008 I discovered and read *Thrilled to Death* by Archibald Hart. I was surprised to find within the context of his book a reasonable critique and challenge to the way many of us do church: "To my Christian readers, I would also like to add that modern worship styles and spiritual practices, when not balanced with contemplative or reflective practices, can also contribute to the hijacking of the brain's pleasure system."

Reading that quote for the first time last year, I had an epiphany. Now I know why I feel drawn to those quiet preludes in the local Episcopal church. I am like a person whose body is short on potassium and thus craves the relief a banana can bring, or a person craving vitamin D who feels the warmth of the sun on her neck and thinks, *Wow, I need to do this more often!* Preludes and what they stand for—quiet, peace, centeredness and the like—are necessary ingredients to a healthy spiritual life. They are among the means—the vitamins—necessary for a life of centered peace.

Unfortunately, reflective times in corporate worship have not been a priority in most contemporary worship services, which are dominated by high stimulation designed to keep the attention of people who are often not otherwise interested in worship. Fortunately, though, there is a renaissance happening across the country that is bringing corporate forms of contemplative practices back into our churches.

Hart helps us create a well-rounded way of seeing all the constituent parts of our lives as a seamless and connected whole. In the midst of all the variety in our life, including work, family, social activities, hobbies and so forth, he teaches us we also need to balance our lives with private mediation and corporate worship. Hart recommends Christian meditation and times of quiet contemplation and concentration focusing on the presence of God. He says too many of us are addicted to extreme forms of stimulation, bored with the ordinary, and developing widespread cases of *anhedonia* (the inability to experience pleasure from the typical events of life). Hart says we are being thrilled to death by our endless pursuit of pleasure, and that in so doing we are becoming incapable of experiencing the very pleasure we seek.

Hart says anhedonia is true of the church too. Contrary to more liturgical traditions, many evangelicals prefer a worship style that is full of intensity and is stimulation driven. They want an *elevating fix* at church, not a contemplative downer. But, Hart says,

> I need to point out that a stimulation-driven spirituality is not conducive to lowered stress and tension or deeper transformation. In fact, many seek a fix when they go to church precisely because they are so stressed out all week that they cannot stand any lowering of their arousal on the weekend. It just puts them into a post-adrenaline bad humor. Unfortunately, many churches don't teach and allow for contemplative practices, so Christians aren't integrating them into their life. A highly stressed lifestyle

finds low arousal discomforting, so our evangelical mantra has become "Bring on the excitement, and I'll go to church!"

I know this is true for both sides of the pulpit. I have both demanded loads of excitement in order to attend church, and I have tried to provide the same for others. Yet I don't know of a single pastor who didn't give a whit about spiritual transformation and said, "I know what I'll do, I'll just create the most exciting church I can to reach people who actually have no intention of changing." No, far from it.

Rather, our overemphasis on stimulation and excitement may come from a desire to connect with our present culture. We who care about evangelism know that we catch fish on their terms, not ours. But this can be a genius bit of missiology or the road to compromise. All evangelism is contextual. Thus the challenge for the church is to be simultaneously geared to our times while being anchored to the Rock, Jesus, and the narrative and trajectory of Scripture. Speaking only for myself, I have to admit that I have erred on the side of trying desperately to provide enough excitement to get people to come to church. I now regret that I may have been inadvertently working against my own passionately stated mission: to make followers of Jesus.

I need to repractice church, and I believe others will find this helpful too. We need to find ways to authentically connect preludes and other contemplative church-based practices into a life of centered peace, which is a powerful form of salt, light and evangelism in our day. For instance, sabbath can be a model for connecting previously existing spiritual strength to the everyday affairs of our life.

PRELUDE AS MINI-SABBATH:
WORKING FROM A PREEXISTING REST

Some may be wondering why *centered peace* is such a big deal. Isn't it the luxury of people going through an easy time in life? No. It is much more profound and central to the well-lived human life. Centered peace implies a deep and abiding form of confidence in Jesus and his care for the whole world, including us. Centered peace, and the ability to act and live from it, underlies the teachings of Jesus:

> Are you tired? Worn out? Burned out on religion? Come to me. Get away with me and you'll recover your life. I'll show you how to take a real rest. Walk with me and work with me—watch how I do it. Learn the unforced rhythms of grace. I won't lay anything heavy or ill-fitting on you. Keep company with me and you'll learn to live freely and lightly. (Matthew 11:28-30)

> What I'm trying to do here is to get you to relax, to not be so preoccupied with *getting,* so you can respond to God's *giving.* People who don't know God and the way he works fuss over these things, but you know both God and how he works. Steep your life in God-reality, God-initiative, God-provisions. Don't worry about missing out. You'll find all your everyday human concerns will be met. (Matthew 6:31-33)

> Peace I leave with you; my peace I give you. I do not give to you as the world gives. Do not let your hearts be troubled and do not be afraid. (John 14:27 NIV)

> I've told you all this so that trusting me, you will be unshakable and assured, deeply at peace. In this godless world you will continue to experience difficulties. But

take heart! I've conquered the world. (John 16:33)

Peace be with you! As the Father has sent me, I am send-ing you. (John 20:21 NIV)

Note the last text: *peace* precedes being sent or flung into the realities of life—as the word for *send* can mean. This is a crucial distinction for our spiritual formation: work happens best within a context of rest or sabbath. This is not the place for a long exploration of the history and meaning of sabbath. But to get going on the idea of preludes being mini-sabbaths, we need a brief reminder of the essence of sabbath in order for it to cre-ate in us an orientation to a habit of life, a rhythm of living in which work flows from rest. Sabbath is simply a weekly day of rest and worship. It comes from the Hebrew *shabbat*, which means "to cease." This word is used in the seventh day of cre-ation when God ceased or rested from his work.

Though sabbath rest is one of the Ten Commandments, Western Christians are not deeply committed to its observation and remembrance. We might do well to ask ourselves two ques-tions: Why don't I value the sabbath the way I do the prohibi-tions against stealing or murder? It seems optional at best. Why do I feel little impetus to obey it? Maybe we have substituted entertainment for real rest!

Maybe our various addictions to stimulants of all kinds fool us into thinking that we really do not need rest or the deep, hu-man refreshment that is a byproduct of sincere, humble wor-ship? Whatever the case, my surprising affinity for preludes and the challenges set forward by Archibald Hart have com-pelled me to find a way to work *from rest.*

I resonate with the way Eugene Peterson puts work and rest into perspective: "Work does not take us away from God; it continues the work of God through us. Sabbath and work are not in opposition; Sabbath and work are integrated parts of an organic whole. Either apart from the other is crippled."

I find hints of the first part of the balance I seek in preludes, and I find structure for it in sabbath. Putting the two together, I discover the basis for an integrated life of centered peace, which subsequently enables me to be an emissary of peace within my daily routines and to the people I meet each day. The last thing I want is to be more religious, especially if *religious* means the opposite of what Peterson advocates—practices that remain disconnected from our work.

THE ENEMIES OF REST

Richard Foster, who I deeply admire as someone who practices working from rest, observes, "In contemporary society our Adversary majors in three things: noise, hurry, and crowds." Because that is surely true, we desperately need quiet time. But Foster also knows the contemplative life is not solitary. Rather, it connects us well to God, to other spiritual practices of Christianity and to the rest of life. It prepares us for the compassionate life (social justice), the virtuous life (holiness), the evangelical life (Word centered), the charismatic life (Spirit centered) and the incarnational life (the sacramental life). Peterson notes, "All our ancestors agree that without silence and stillness there is no spirituality, no God-attentive, God-responsive life."

Here is an interesting and revealing question related to the practice of preludes: is *quiet time* a work or a grace? Do we imagine that God bestows grace in payment for devotional regularity? We often think, *If I read my Bible and pray enough, somehow I will pull the right lever with God and he will respond!*

This line of thought leads to a bigger challenge: misunderstanding grace. All of God's actions and inactions—his patience, his withholding judgments and so forth—are of grace. Creation is an act of grace; all of the ongoing human abilities to live and breath are acts of grace. Grace does not have to do merely with fixing the problem of sin. Once we see this, we see that quiet times are themselves graces, the means to connect with the mercy and power of God. They are not *properly* understood as works.

Think of the rhythm of Jesus' life, who easily and frequently moved from private times of prayer to times of public teaching, healing and confronting. In these routine times of solitude and quiet, was Jesus working to earn something from his Father? Or were all the actions of Jesus' life, public and private, motivated and energized by the grace of God? I think it is the latter.

This understanding has freed me in numerous ways. It never crosses my mind to wonder how many chapters I should read today or how long I should pray. These types of questions have been replaced—repracticed—by a life in which prayer is never far away, never confined to the next morning, and thinking about Scripture is foundational for all of life, not just early mornings.

I experience repracticed quiet time this way: as I pay attention to the people and events of my day, my life is full of divine appointments and divine interruptions. This produces the desire and the need to have daily uninterrupted times of focus on God. But it is important to see this as practical and functional, not an attempt to earn anything from God or to get him to do something for me. It's all part of one contiguous whole. That *whole* is my life lived before God in public activity and private contemplation, prayer and study.

So when sitting quietly in a sanctuary, thinking and praying while beautiful music plays, I know I have only ascended the diving board. Once the benediction has been pronounced, I walk out the door ready to splash into the realities of life. I then experience a life of centered peace, working from a place of rest gained from engaging in the spiritual practice of prelude.

3

Singing the Doxology

Radiating the Glory of God

"There is ultimately no justification for a private piety that
doesn't work out in actual mission, just as there is ultimately
no justification for people who use their activism in the social, cultural or political sphere as a screen to prevent them
from facing the same challenges within their own lives—the
challenge, that is, of God's Kingdom, of Jesus' lordship, and
of the Spirit's empowering. If the Gospel isn't transforming
you, how do you know it will transform anything else?"

N. T. WRIGHT

As an adolescent I often pondered the various Christian
symbols covering the front wall of my Methodist church. To my
untrained eye they were more like a secret code than cherished
ancient symbols of faith. From where I sat, the display looked
like a giant shadow box hung on the wall in the shape of a ca-

thedral arch. Within the arch each compartment contained an icon meant to remind knowledgeable believers of a treasured era or aspect of Christianity.

On many occasions I recall being pulled back from the symbols to the worship service by the organist playing the introductory notes of the doxology. I loved the engaging, simple melody and the sincere voices of Christians harmonizing without strain or self-indulgence. The tune stuck in my head and remains there to this day. These days I find myself singing it at various times: observing sunrises or sunsets, or viewing beautiful landscapes, or being thankful for just about any good thing from God. At those moments my heart and mind soar:

Praise God from whom all blessings flow;
Praise him all creatures here below;
Praise him above you heavenly hosts;
Praise Father, Son and Holy Ghost.

This chapter has two foci: (1) the glory of God and (2) that we are created in God's image. We will explore how through repracticing the doxology, we radiate the glory of God in the routines of our life.

Doxology is not simply a part of a worship service—it is a manner or way of life. It is a part of what the old-school Christian writers called our *walk* or our *conversation*. This is true because God is not just transcendent (wholly other and distinct from us) but is also immanent (near or close to us). Thus while Christians sing the doxology in church, it is helpful to keep in mind that Jesus not only taught us to bring glory to God, he also taught us to pray, "your will be done on earth [that is in and through my life] as it is in heaven."

Doxology is a word that connotes the overall quality, the most pronounced characteristic or feature of a life. If correct thinking about God (theology) leads to the right worship of God (doxology), then doxology leads to a life that radiates the praise of God in a way that others experience as for their own good.

Using terms like *doxology* and *radiate* can sound overwhelming, maybe even impossible. But I will give you a couple of examples of lives that are radiant in very simple, doable ways that bless and encourage others. These brief snippets of stories come from e-mails that were sent to me from participants in a pilot program I ran for Three Is Enough Groups.

> During our first meeting at lunch an older Armenian woman (pretty safe guess because we were in Glendale, CA) in her 70s came up to us and said, "It's so nice to see men get together and talk and have such a joyous time together."
>
> Because we've been meeting in public places (Corner Bakery, coffee places), a girl came up last night and asked us what we were doing. She said she was a new Christian and that it was great to "see godly men doing what we were doing," even though she had no clue what that was. It gave us a chance to meet her and pray for her.
>
> After meeting for three weeks . . . one of our members was going out of town and would be returning just a few hours before our next meeting. We asked him if the meeting should be postponed or rescheduled. He replied, "I *need* this group and we are definitely meeting at our regular time." He then shared how much the group meant to him and how he values being connected to us, growing closer to God, how his prayers are being answered, and

the significant impact of the TIE service component in such a short amount of time.

Our TIE group has chosen to pray for each other's marriages and also for couples that are in our circle of influence. First we discussed how marriage in general is under attack and how each of us would appreciate the support from the group in terms of prayer. The next week we shared personal struggles and asked for prayer in the areas that each man had responsibility to change. Last week we shared breakthroughs that other couples in our circles of influence had experienced during the week since we started praying. . . . [O]ne man moved back in the home with his family, another man gave his life to the Lord. [E]ach of us are amazed and grateful at what is happening in the arena of marriages.

These stories not only capture well the premise of Three Is Enough Groups, they also fittingly articulate the notion I have in mind when I use the word *radiate*. I do not envision grunting effort or weird religious legalism. Just trust Jesus on this one: a light *cannot* be hid. Once we are in touch with giving glory to God, it automatically turns on a light—kind of like one of those light-sensitive wall switches that *automatically* turns on the lamp as the sun goes down.

DOXOLOGY IN THE DIRT OF EVERYDAY LIFE

Going back out into the street, reengaging with real life after singing the doxology in church, can make us forget what we believe and how we felt while we were singing. To exude the glory of God requires that we have some idea of what that could look like—we need a vision for it, someone who has modeled it.

Jesus is of course the most complete model. But if we view him as only a "spiritual" or divine being, Jesus doesn't do well as a role model. Many Christians can't imagine Jesus with dirt under his fingernails. So we end up thinking that Jesus is a great savior of souls and a revealer of spiritual secrets, but when it comes to making a living in a dog-eat-dog world or of living in a quarreling family, Jesus is not much use.

In the New Testament book of Romans, Paul is amazed that in spite of the sin of the human race, God is not vindictive but showers us with his grace through Jesus. In Romans 11:33-36 Paul breaks out in praise to God, he gushes over with doxology:

> Oh, the depth of the riches of the wisdom and knowledge
>   of God!
>   How unsearchable his judgments,
>   and his paths beyond tracing out!
> "Who has known the mind of the Lord?
>   Or who has been his counselor?"
> "Who has ever given to God,
>   that God should repay him?"
> For from him and through him and to him are all things.
>   To him be the glory forever! Amen. (NIV)

In this doxological praise to God, Paul is trying to find adequate words to express his amazement at the plan of God to redeem both Israel and Gentiles through Jesus. And his doxology cannot be reduced to "pie in the sky" because chapters 9–11 address God's plan for humans in this life. Paul is blown away not by heavenly visions by what he sees happening all around him. The Gentiles are in! It is like the end of the hide-and-seek games we played as kids. At the end we would yell

"Ally, ally, in come free!" Whoever will place their faith—their confidence and trust—in Jesus, is now part of God's plan.

In Romans, Paul surveys the intention of God, the expression of that intention in creation, the Fall, law, grace, the person and work of Jesus, his own struggle to work all this out, and God's plan for Israel and the Gentiles. Maybe at Romans 11:32, he put his pen down, leaned back in his chair, rubbed his face and thought, *Wow. This is truly amazing stuff!*

RADIATING THE LIGHT OF GOD IS A CHOICE

When interacting with Jesus, a stark reality often dawns on us. Jesus is like the working lights in a restaurant. Throughout the dinner hour, the lights are low, providing the atmosphere for quiet conversation in an out-of-the-way booth. But all night, food falls to the carpet: sourdough bread crumbs, pasta sauce and pieces of lettuce. Though, by the end of the night, there is food everywhere, the low lights disguise this fact.

But when the last group has paid the bill, left the tip, put on their coats and pushed their way out the glass door, the bright working lights go on. Everything is exposed to the light so that the honest and diligent restaurateur can clean up for the next day.

Jesus had something like this in mind when he said to Nicodemus:

> This is the crisis we're in: God-light streamed into the world, but men and women everywhere ran for the darkness. They went for the darkness because they were not really interested in pleasing God. Everyone who makes a practice of doing evil, addicted to denial and illusion, hates God-light and won't come near it, fearing a painful exposure. But anyone working and living in truth and re-

ality welcomes God-light so the work can be seen for the God-work it is. (John 3:21)

It's true, isn't it? Why do we so often resonate with darkness and fear the light? Darkness is a place to hide, like Adam and Eve hiding from God in the Garden of Eden. In response, God called out: "Adam, where are you?" This question implies God has always wanted to be with and interact with his in-trouble, and thus embarrassed, children. But since God is light, being around him brings our life into bright clearness. It takes guts—what the Bible calls faith or belief—to trust, to have confidence that God will do good to us when we come into the light with sticky evidence on our lips and fingers, showing with certainty that we have been playing in the cookie jar God told us to stay away from.

Here is a thought from Dallas Willard about radiating the nature of God, which glows with powerful self-evident truth:

> The people to whom we minister and speak will not recall 99 percent of what we say to them, but they will never forget the kind of persons we are. This is certainly true of influential ministers in my own past. The quality of our souls will indelibly touch others for good or for ill. So we must never forget that the most important thing happening at any moment, in the midst of all our ministerial duties, is the kind of persons we are becoming.

When I read something like this, I immediately feel like I could go a year without reading another sentence and just focus on *the kind of person I am becoming.* Focusing on that thought for a good while would enable us to repractice doxology in such a way that our actual lives would emit the goodness and glory of God.

RADIATING IS NOT JUST FOR SUPER-SAINTS

The stories I retold earlier in the chapter were intended to make radiating doable through the spiritual practice of doxology. But some are undoubtedly unconvinced and are still wondering how we can radiate anything of God. *Aren't we all just worms, addicted, crummy, selfish bottom feeders?* I've had my moments when I can relate. But in order to repractice doxology, glorifying God in our everyday schedules, we must discover the dignity and value of the human person.

Observing fifty years of cultural development, it is staggering to note how much we have lost of what it means to be a person, to be real, to be distinctly male or female, and to be humans made in the image of God. Willard comes again to our aid: "Emphasis on the wickedness and neediness of the human being . . . tends to submerge our awareness of our greatness and our worth to God." Here is a vital bit of theology for all those wanting to connect with God in a way that radiates his presence to others: Our story, the biblical human story, starts in the bright light of the precreation intention of God, not the fall into sin. It doesn't start with the darkness of Genesis gone wrong. The preincarnate Son of Man, who exudes the glory of God, is who we look to, not Adam.

Can we agree that when people have "I'm nothing" as their central view of self, it does not produce the growth in grace we are seeking? Can we also admit that the other side of the same coin, the effort to make the children of boomers and society in general feel good about themselves has not worked either? To repractice doxology in the routines of our lives, we need a third way, a deep and confident knowledge that rather than being *nothing* (and then misleadingly built up) we are a *splendid ruin*—people marvelous by design and purpose, but presently damaged.

We do not have to have a degree in Old Testament theology to imagine the magnitude of what God might have had in mind for his creation. If flowers, art, a forest or an ocean sunset sometimes stun you, imagine what God had in mind for humans. We can't get there from *nothingness*. We start with something *grand* and only later acknowledge what a *wreck* human life has become. As we consider repracticing the glory of God in our work, we must keep this grandeur in mind.

If a little Peter Pan pixy dust, as in that movie, can get someone across town, imagine what a modest bit of God's glory can do for our life and for those we have contact with. *Radiating* sounds big and bold, maybe even overreaching. But actually God has already done most of the work. To repractice doxology we do not need to get too worked up about ourselves or get too self-focused.

Here are a couple of more unpretentious terms that might help us relax. Jesus says of his followers, "You are the salt of the earth. . . . You are the light of the world" (Matthew 5:13-14 NIV). This is "radiating" on ground level. We can do that.

Moving from doxology to radiating a life is actually quite natural. It's quite difficult to hide light, to hide a city on hill. A city on a hill does not make special efforts to be seen—it just *is*. It radiates naturally. Often, when flying home at night, I can see the lights of Salt Lake City or Las Vegas. I can even see them through thin cloud cover. As Jesus asserted, it's hard to hide a city—even one on a flat desert.

I like to sleep in a very dark room. Even the smallest bit of light radiating through the shade has the power to distract me from sleep. Likewise, our smallest bits of light have the power to reorient the lives of others. I learned this in a dramatic way. While I was ministering at the Vineyard in Anaheim, we had a blackout during one of our services. A automobile accident knocked out a power line to our building. There were approximately three thousand people in the room and close to a thousand children in the area behind the sanctuary. For a reason I cannot remember, the emergency lights failed too.

Sitting in the front row of the church, I was only a dozen steps from the hallway leading to the children, but the darkness was so overwhelming and disorienting that it was difficult groping my way there.

When I finally reached the door that led to a long hallway, I saw a mother who had a small flashlight on her key chain had beat me to the door and was making her way to her children. Her small light didn't illumine the whole hallway, but it reoriented the whole scary moment for me. Soon others found emergency flashlights in the classrooms, and still others shined their car headlights through the classroom windows. We got all the kids out to safety.

After about five or ten minutes I made my way back to the sanctuary. It looked like a 1960s rock concert, as all the baby boomers had gotten out their Bic lighters and were waving them around as if "Hey Jude" was being performed by the Beatles. As funny as that was, what I still remember twenty years later is the enormous power of that mom's flashlight to bring hope and orientation to a seriously unnerving moment. The spiritual practice of doxology has this effect. The light of Christ in a worshiping human being cannot be hid.

THE DOXOLOGY WAS ONCE CONTEMPORARY CHRISTIAN MUSIC

I'll bet I'm not the only one for whom the Doxology comes to mind at the sight or sound of God's creation or his work in our daily life. Let me repeat it here:

Praise God from whom all blessings flow;
> Praise him all creatures here below;
> Praise him above you heavenly hosts;
> Praise Father, Son and Holy Ghost. Amen.

Thomas Ken wrote those lines in 1674. They were a final refrain to three hymns he composed. That means millions of Christians have sung those words billions of times over the last three centuries. Apparently Ken wrote them under controversial conditions. In his day it was thought that only words of Scripture were appropriate lyrics for songs sung in church. Though the Doxology seems old and formal to us, Ken ironically wrote these words for the youth of his day. What is so alluring about them? What is their remarkable power for edification?

Praise God from whom all blessings flow. The Doxology's first line is not just appropriate at the birth of a baby, the setting of the sun or some similar wonder, we can use it at all times to glorify God. These words ground us in a way of life in the Spirit. And only grounded people have the cash, so to speak, to spend on radiating the presence of God to others. People not in touch with the glory, which in Hebrew means "weight," of God float. They are insecure and therefore often self-focused. Such people have a very difficult time shining in ways that are good for others.

Praise him all creatures here below. The second line is an invitation to a unique way of living. Praise is the correct response of a creature who sees the glory of God. Doxology goes beyond the knowledge gained from study. Doxology wells up from *experiencing* the truth and goodness of God. The attitudes necessary for and normative to a life of praise are spelled out in the apostle Paul's description of love in 1 Corinthians 13 (i.e., "love is patient . . . kind . . . not proud . . .") and in his portrayal of love as the chief fruit of the Spirit in Galatians 5 (i.e., "love, joy, peace, patience . . ."). Praise comes from and leads to devotion to God and to his purposes on earth. Praise springs from grateful humility.

Praise him above you heavenly hosts. When we give praise to God, we enter into a long and storied past. The heavenly hosts have praised God for longer than we know how to count time. Asking the heavenly hosts to praise God, as the third line of the Doxology does, is a way of asserting how much God deserves praise. The heavenly hosts know with much more clarity than "we who see though a glass darkly" that God is worthy of our praise.

Praise Father, Son and Holy Ghost. Allusions to the Trinity in songs or poetry like the fourth line of the Doxology point us to the eternal and always-existing totality of God. Evoking the Trinity reminds worshipers of the full disclosure of God, which in turn produces grateful worship to this God who lovingly makes himself known to us. The three persons of the Trinity call to mind all of God's work: creation, redemption and power for a new life of loving obedience.

Amen. Amen comes from a Hebrew word that means "truly" or "I give assent" or "I agree." In the Doxology it means "so be it," "let it happen," "may it come about in just this way," "it is sure to take place," "Yes. Yes. Yes."

Anything that happens with a view to bringing glory to God is a form of doxology. And it leads to good things for others—like in this story from a Three Is Enough Group:

> The premise of the group, as explained on the podcasts that I got from the website, really struck a chord with me. It gave me a tangible, applicable method to put Christ first and begin to build a precedent, and an outline for my spiritual life. It worked on my thoughts throughout my "normal" daily life where I began to become more mindful of the needs around me. My interactions with people I deal with during the day changed as I began to think "how can I bless them," or "They look a bit down, let me lift them up in prayer."

What if you took a spiritual risk and brought your little light out from under a basket one night and the wind blew it out (meaning it didn't go well)? It counts. Why? Because you had the *intention* of bringing glory to God for the sake of others. In so doing you were cooperating with God's intention for you.

When we cooperate with God, we take steps down the right path to repractice doxology. We connect with God's light, which gives our life light. Like a city on a hill our light cannot—and will not—be hid.

Scripture Reading

Embodying the Story

"God did not give the Bible so we could master him or it;
God gave the Bible so we could live it, so we could be mastered by it.
The moment we think we have mastered it, we have
failed to be readers of the Bible."

SCOT McKNIGHT

My daughter, Carol, is a good example of a young person trying to discover and live in the overarching story of God. She might not be good at Bible trivia, but she is good at having and expressing the heart of God for the least, the last and the left out. Carol cares about injustice, poverty and the social ills of Africa. I have no idea where she got it. Neither her mother nor I have ever said a word to her about it. A few years ago we did see the movie *Invisible Children*, which may have started it for her. All I know is that almost every day, while most other kids are sporting their best Abercrombie & Fitch or Aeropostale,

Carol is wearing a One sweatshirt or an Invisible Children T-shirt. This past summer she had a garage sale and gave the proceeds of $500 to the Invisible Children organization. To her surprise, a few days later she received a beautiful handwritten note in the mail:

> Dear Carol,
>
> We at Invisible Children want to thank you for all of your hard work and compassion for the children of Northern Uganda. We're so impressed with you and your parents are justifiably proud! ☺ Because of your kindness, remarkable things are happening!
>
> With Hope,
> The IC Team

I should be quick to point out that neither our son, Jonathan, nor Carol are church-going, Bible-carrying Christians. They both are struggling through life, like most young people, trying to find a faith of their own—not simply the faith of their parents. I point this out for two reasons: first, I don't want to brag about my kids, and second, they, while unsure about church, represent those who have a pretty good idea of what God is up to in terms of the big narrative of Scripture: loving God and others as ourselves.

READING THE BIBLE

The fact is that the amount of Scripture read in most church services is shrinking. Up until recently, I haven't attended a church that had multiple Scripture readings as part of its worship. I come from a tradition in which the only text read is that which the preacher is going to speak on. I cherish my church background, but I find it interesting that

> the calendars for the public reading of Scripture have re-
> sulted in Anglicans hearing more of the Word of God in
> their services than any other major branch of Christen-
> dom . . . [and that] more of the Bible is read in Anglican
> churches in one month than is read in two years in most
> other churches.

Why is this important? Because we are trying to embody
the story of the Bible, not simply note or even memorize its
propositional statements. The lectionary of most Western liturgical churches is laid out so that the readings from the Old
Testament, Psalms, Epistles and Gospels tell the story of the
Bible once a year. I believe that the more of the story we hear,
the better our worldview and lifestyles will be shaped by the
story of God.

THE BIBLE: CAN YOU ACTUALLY TRUST IT?

In the last year I have been given two beautiful leather-bound
Bibles—and I cherish them both. One was given me at my ordination to the Anglican deaconate and the other at my ordination
to Holy Orders—the moment I was set apart for ministry within
the Anglican Church. Glancing at them on the bookshelf, I notice that I have a shelf overflowing with various translations of
the Bible. I have so many that some are piled on the top of others. (I just counted; there are thirty-six of them!) I guess that is
what happens when you have been a student and collector of the
Bible since disco and the Bee Gees were a big deal.

On the other hand, over this same thirty-year period, the
Bible has fallen on hard times. This is hard to imagine because

there are Bibles of every color and design, for every purpose and target group. There are multitudes of *translations* and still more *commentaries* on the text of the Bible. Some churchgoers complain of having a bellyache from being overfed the *meat* of the Word; others grumble that they are only getting *milk* of the Word and not the *deeper* things of God. Thoughtful church historians have commented that since the Reformation and the invention of the printing press everyone has been given equal access to the Bible, but that this has led to divisive ways of reading the Bible, which has in turn led to 38,000 denominations! This can't be what God had in mind.

Obviously owning a Bible is not our problem. The problem is we don't know how to read it. Or we don't trust our readings of it any longer. Or maybe we trust *our* reading but not *theirs*. Some have become deeply suspicious of the Bible: How can anyone believe in a God who does (or doesn't do) such and such, as we see in the Bible. Today, many church outsiders no longer wonder whether the Bible is true and accurate, but whether it is a source of goodness or evil.

With negative ideas like these and others surrounding the Bible today, we might be tempted to settle for people merely reading their Bibles. But we know too much for that. We know that if the Bible is to have a useful place in our hyper-modern, technological but philosophically postmodern culture, we are going to have to engage Scripture as the source of a story to be embodied in our actual life.

HOW TO READ THE BIBLE CORRECTLY
AND WITH GOOD OUTCOMES

Not long ago my Three Is Enough group had a discussion of

chapter seven of Dallas Willard's *Hearing God*, which is about hearing God through the Scriptures. My group resonated strongly with the following passage on reading the Bible in a way that produces embodied goodness:

> We will be spiritually safe in our use of the Bible if we follow a simple rule: *Read it with a submissive attitude.* Read with a readiness to surrender all you are—all your plans, opinions, possessions, positions. Study as intelligently as possible, with all available means, but never study merely to find the truth and especially not just to prove something wrong. Subordinate your desire to *find* the truth to your desire to *do* it, to act it out!

Thus our vision of the best way to read the Bible need not be of ourselves surrounded by a stack of Bible study tools—as helpful as they are. (I use them all the time.) Rather than a stack of books, maybe we should envision a stack of papers that contain plans, blueprints, strategies, structures and vows for embodying what we are reading. For, as N. T. Wright says, "new life in the Spirit, in obedience to the lordship of Jesus Christ, should produce radical transformation of behavior in the present life, *anticipating* the life to come even though we know we shall never be complete and whole until then."

I know many Christians who hate the idea of *obedience*. I do too, sometimes. I do not like being told what to do. Normally, I can keep this instinct at bay. But I wonder if I am not a little too easy on myself; perhaps I am kidding myself. For most of us obedience is something we know or believe we cannot accomplish. Thus it leaves us not wanting to do much with our religion. It leaves us in the classic push-pull relationship with

God—pushing him away in fear of failure and rebuke, but pulling him close in other moments of sincere love or need. But what if we reimagined obedience in a way that allowed us to repractice it? What if obedience becomes the joy of embodying a story we value—like the joy experienced by a child who has learned to play basketball or the violin?

Christians tend to read the Bible as a book of doctrines, with the occasional well-known story thrown in. But in this way of reading Scripture we lose the context, a sense of our setting in history and God's purpose for creating humans, Israel and the church. When this is lost, missing too is the reason and motivation to work the words of Jesus into our lives.

Though I've been reading the Bible for decades, when I read very familiar passages I learn something new. How can this be when the text remains the same? I change from day to day, and the world, the context in which I read Scripture, alters constantly. Thus reading the Bible is not merely about correct interpretation but also about continuously returning to it to find a way to *live* with it.

When we see an intense movie, we have to *live with it* in the sense that it haunts our life for a day, a week or longer. I have viewed some movies like *Amazing Grace, Hotel Rwanda* and *Luther* over and over again. Why? Because I've forgotten the story? No, I want to immerse myself in the stories because I want to learn to live in them; I want them to rub off on me so that I care more for the sick, the abused and those living under tyranny. The job of the Bible is not merely to give us an accurate notion of God, though it is the best place to look for such help. The Bible's most powerful role is to illumine the *practices* associated with being a follower of the God we find in the Bible.

KINGDOM, MISSION, EMBODIMENT

No serious Christian would admit, "Nah, why would I want to *embody* the story of the Bible. I think I'll settle for merely reading it." Those of us who have been reading the Bible for some time know that James 1:22 ("Do not merely listen to the word, and so deceive yourselves. Do what it says"; NIV) says such a decision is way off base. Nevertheless, embodying Scripture often isn't our top priority. So are we trapped? Are we caught between not actually intending to embody the story of Scripture and knowing that we can't ignore obedient embodiment? Maybe a little work on the word *embody* will help us get going.

The term *embody* first entered my thinking when I read the important book *Missional Church*, which was written to help mainline churches find a missional ecclesiology that had at its core a vision to re-present the reign of God. (Ironically, it became a driving force within the emerging church.) The word *embody* is a fundamental notion from the book that caused me to rethink how to best read the Bible.

A brief overview of *Missional Church* will help us repractice Bible reading as embodying its story. The church derives its meaning from the mission of God as expressed in Jesus and his gospel of the kingdom: the good news that the rule and reign of God, the expressed action of God, is now present with us in a special way and will one day be forever consummated on earth. Thus the church is created by the action of God. The church is the instrument or means of the reign of God on earth; it represents the rule of God as an agent, a sign and a foretaste of the coming consummated kingdom. The church carries out these activities by announcing, embodying and demonstrating the gospel of the kingdom.

As I've thought about this missional paradigm over the past ten years and tried to come up with a simple, take-home concept for frustrated seekers like me, I've landed on "embody the story of Scripture." But what does it mean to *embody* something? To embody can mean to incarnate, to make visible or present, to make concrete or perceptible, to incorporate or to personify.

A LIVING, VISIBLE EMBODIMENT

Thus our conversation now moves to *how* we engage the practice of Scripture reading in order to make its story visible and present in our bodily living. How do we make it perceptible and concrete in the attitudes and actions of our lives such that it could be said that we personify the main plot of the Bible? Isn't *living* much more interesting and challenging than merely *studying*? I think I now know one reason the Bible has fallen on hard times: as interesting as it is, it is not compelling enough to stick with unless it becomes the substance of our life story and basis for a lifelong journey of repentance and alignment to its story as followers of Jesus.

I've often commented to friends that the introductions Eugene Peterson wrote for the individual books of the Bible in *The Message* are worth the price of the whole Bible! This comment from his introduction to James is typical—and spot on for our present topic: "Wisdom is not primarily knowing the truth, although it certainty includes that; it is skill in *living*. For, what good is a truth if we don't know how to *live* it? What good is an intention if we can't sustain it?"

When we read the Bible in this manner, it's like a prized document that tells us how to participate in something we long to do, but which is still not 100 percent clear to us. For instance, imagine someone trying to learn about baseball but only knowing where three of the bases go for sure because pages are missing from the rules booklet. Or imagine learning a piece of lovely music only to discover the last twenty or thirty bars are missing.

Once we begin to read the Bible with the enthusiasm of athletes and musicians who have discovered secrets to their sport or art and gain their predisposition to act on it, we will no longer be mere readers but will *embody* the Word of God. Rather than submitting to the Bible *against our wills*, as it were, we love and value its Author so much that we eagerly seek to know what he is up to in redeeming his creation.

Reading the Bible (or any other spiritual discipline or means of grace, for that matter) was never intended to be abstract or academic. Eugene Peterson is an expert guide to the preferred way of reading the Bible, the proper approach to spiritual formation:

> What we often consider to be the concerns of the spiritual life—ideas, truths, prayers, promises, beliefs—are never in the Christian gospel permitted to have a life of their own apart from particular persons and actual places. Biblical spirituality/religion has a low tolerance for "great ideas" or "sublime truths" or "inspirational thoughts" apart from the people and places in which they occur. God's great love and purposes for us are all worked out in the messes in our kitchen and backyards, in storms and sins, blue skies, the daily work and dreams of our common lives. . . .
>
> The opening scene in the resurrection of Jesus occurs in the workplace. Mary Magdalene and the other women

were on their way to work when they encountered and embraced the resurrection of Jesus. I'm prepared to contend that the primary location for spiritual formation is the workplace. . . .

Story is the most natural way of enlarging and deepening our sense of reality, and then enlisting us as participants in it. . . . They then welcome us in. Stories are verbal acts of hospitality. . . .

The biblical way is not to present us a moral code and tell us "Live up to this," nor is it to set out a system of doctrine and say, "Think like this and you will live well." The biblical way is to tell a story that takes place on solid ground, is peopled with men and women that we recognize as being much like us, and then to invite us, *"Live into this. This is what it looks like to be human. This is what is involved in entering and maturing as human beings."*

Can you see how God and the Bible may have engendered a bad reputation he and his book do not deserve? I am pretty sure the average person on the street thinks that God cares more about our capacity to grasp ideas, thoughts and truths, or our agreement with obscure doctrines—the reverse of what Peterson says. This is how far we have gotten from embodying the simple story line of the Bible.

EMBODIMENT: DISCOVERING FOOD FOR THE SOUL

The Gospel of John tells a well-known story of Jesus being on long walk with his disciples through Samaria, whose people the Jews despised. When Jesus and the disciples drew near a Samaritan town, Jesus stopped at the well. His disciples went into town to get something to eat, and a Samaritan woman came to the well with her water jar. A vitally important conversation with Jesus ensued (see John 4:10-26).

When the disciples arrived at the well with lunch, the conversation between Jesus and the woman was ending and the woman went back to the town. Stunned and a little embarrassed to see Jesus talking to a Samaritan woman, the disciples nervously evade the issue and say, in effect, "Hey, Jesus, you've got to be starving; we walked all morning, then you had to wait while we went for food. Why don't you eat something?"

Jesus answers, "I have food to eat you know nothing about" (v. 32). "The food that keeps me going is that I do the will of the One who sent me" (v. 34). (Can't you just hear one of the guys muttering under his breath in the back of the pack, "Well then why did we go all to way to town to get food!") In saying this, Jesus meant that he finds satisfaction and delight through his conversation with the Samaritan woman and in the wider drama of what it is accomplishing in her community, which makes food relatively unappealing in the moment. We have all experienced this at some point. Imagine thoroughly cleaning the garage or reorganizing a cupboard on a Saturday morning, and before you know it it's almost noon and you have not eaten. Being so *focused on* work, you did not even notice that you were hungry.

"The food that keeps me going is that I do the will of the One who sent me" is a statement of priorities. For Jesus, his foremost priority is doing the will of his Father—which may be the best definition of *embody*. In this passage Jesus is simply living in congruity with his own teaching:

> Therefore I tell you, do not worry about your life, what
> you will eat or drink. . . . Is not life more important than

food. . . . So do not worry, saying, "What shall we eat?" or "What shall we drink?" . . . For the pagans run after all these things, and your heavenly Father knows that you need them. But seek first his kingdom and his righteousness, and all these things will be given to you as well. (Matthew 6:25, 31-34 NIV)

One of Jesus' temptations before Satan (Matthew 4:1-17) was to turn rocks into bread. Jesus' refusal to do so illustrates the steadfastness of his commitment and devotion to stay true to his incarnational calling. By overcoming these temptations, Jesus inaugurated a new way of living in which his followers embody the missional narrative of God, not the story offered to us by the devil.

The disciples weren't explicitly tempting Jesus in offering him food. They were concerned friends looking after a friend who found eating too impractical at the moment. But Jesus had a laser-like focus on what his Father was trying to do with this woman from Samaria.

Jesus was sustained and fulfilled by embodying the story of his Father. Of course he ate real food, but in this situation he knew there were more important things happening—an inbreaking of the kingdom of God to the Samaritans. The disciples were oblivious to this because they were focusing on food and the cultural taboo about talking to a woman from Samaria. They were missing a major turning point in redemptive history. The walls between Jews, Gentiles and others were being torn down. What his Father was doing with the Samaritan woman so captured Jesus' attention, was so fulfilling, that he hungered to see what would happen next.

Jesus seemed to enjoy seeing his Father's story unfold before him. It gave his life a sense of adventure. Today, we tend to think that only rock stars, athletes, media people and politicians live truly interesting lives. I doubt the perception is reality. I believe a person could outwardly live a normal, even mundane, life, but because of being born again into the life of the kingdom that same person could live the most interesting life imaginable. That is what God planned for us—to work with him to accomplish his purposes, to steward his creation. This was God's intention for Israel, to be his agents of rescue in a world gone bad, and what he intends for the church, to work with him, as Jesus did, as his agents of forgiveness, healing and deliverance.

HOW ARE WE TO LIVE THE BIBLE TODAY?

Scot McKnight gets right to the point on the opening page of his book *The Blue Parakeet*. If we pay attention to the subtitle of chapter one, it will lead to a different kind of Christian life and new witness in the world: "How, Then, Are We to Live the Bible Today?" Notice he doesn't ask first "How Do We Read the Bible?" Once we have decided to live the Bible, it will shape how we read it. For "living the Bible as story" as McKnight says, is an even more powerful image than applying the Bible. Getting right down to where the rubber tire meets the road, we could not go too far wrong by simply using the following two sentences as a basic operating system:

If you are doing good works, you are reading the Bible aright.

If you are not doing good works, *you are not reading the Bible aright.*

STAINED-GLASS CHRISTIANITY

What then is the connection between reading, story and embodying? This is what I know to be experientially true: Read the Bible enough that you know its story as well as you know your favorite movie. (Some people can recite all the lines to *Monty Python and the Holy Grail*, *A Christmas Story* or *Napoleon Dynamite*.) Steep your imagination in the story of the Bible to such an extent that it both creates the outline of your story and fills in the details moment by moment as you recognize the plot being played out, and the Spirit moving within the people and events of your life.

I have found these questions helpful when reading the Bible: Did the Bible just happen to others, or does it continue to happen? Did Adam and Eve sin, or do we sin? Did Israel get delivered from exile, or do we get delivered too? Did Jesus rise, or do we rise too? The Bible did not just happen to others long ago in a culture we no longer relate to. Biblical content is not just disembodied and timeless truths, principles or precepts. The Bible is not something that comes out of the blue or simply floats above space and time. It is a grounded, historical, real-life narrative. It is like a family scrapbook or photo album bursting with storied explanation of God and his people. We respect the Bible best when we respect the manner in which God gave it—which is narrative, a story for us to embody.

Before reading was prevalent, stained-glass windows were a favored way of telling the story of the Bible. I know, to some people these old and faded objects are no match for computer-generated graphics. But for some of us, to stand in a magnificent edifice such as the thirteenth-century Canterbury Cathedral is a moving experience.

In Canterbury Cathedral, as in other churches and cathedrals, there is a stained-glass window known as "The Poor Man's Bible." This was created to illustrate the teachings of the Bible for a largely illiterate population. Though I am, compared to vast majority of the world, a highly literate person, when I stand before such windows, sunlight flooding through them, I don't see dirty, old, leaded glass. I see a story beckoning me to enter its world; to embody the narrative illuminated by brightly lit glass. I am drawn in.

We will have engaged in the spiritual practice of Scripture reading when we experience the ink of the Bible similarly calling to us—"Come, live in God's story."

Hearing Sermons

An Easy-Yoke Life of Obedience

"The Bible doesn't just inform its hearers about its narrative.
It invites us into it, enfolds us in it, assures us of our membership in it,
and equips us for our tasks in pursuit of its goal."

N. T. WRIGHT

I've been leading Bible studies and preaching since I was a college student. Within the first few weeks of coming to faith, a few of Debbie's (who is now my wife) girlfriends wanted to get together with their boyfriends to learn the Bible. This was not a big deal in the Southern California Jesus movement of the 1970s. The first night we got together, we needed volunteer leaders, and someone picked me to go first. I have no idea how I prepared, what books I consulted or how I outlined the talk. I just know that when I was done, the group said they wanted me to keep giving the talks. I had no idea I had the spiritual gift of teaching. Throughout the ensuing years while studying at Bible school and seminary, and pursuing doctoral studies, I learned all about sermons.

A sermon, sometimes called a homily, is a discourse usually delivered in a religious service. But Moses, Jesus and Peter spoke outside of such a setting. Famously, so did John Wesley and George Whitefield. As the Bible became central to the life of the church during and after the Reformation, sermons took on increased importance in church worship meetings. The basic task of a sermon is to expound on a passage from the Bible, on a bit of theology or on a bit of religious history. The goal is to make these various topics both understandable and edifying—to both inform and form a congregation. The basic structure for a sermon is *observation* (what the text says), *interpretation* (what the text means) and *application* (what to do about it). In this chapter I want to focus on the disconnect between observation, interpretation, application and our daily life.

A big part of my motivation for writing this book is rooted in deep and gnawing intellectual curiosity: Why don't the various aspects of church life produce better results? How does it happen that people can follow and experience profound liturgies for their whole lives and not feel connected to Jesus in a personal way? How can people hear great sermons for dozens of years and yet cheat their customers and cheat on their spouse?

Philip Yancey says, "My deepest doubts about the faith can be summed up in a single question: 'Why doesn't it work?'" In the margin of Yancey's *Soul Survivor,* I wrote, "Me too!" As a leader of pastors, every time I've seen one crash and burn with sex, money or pride, I've wondered, *Why doesn't our faith work?* And when I've watched a parishioner ruin his or her family through foolish behavior, I've asked the same troubling question.

This question is not for the faint of heart. But it demands an answer. Here is my best shot: The problem has little to do with our liturgy, sermons, Sunday school curricula or any other aspect of church life. These elements are common means of God's instruction, power and grace. Our problem has more to do with two other things: first, we have no place, no story and no context with which to act on anything we might hear or receive; second, in our pseudo-religious society we lack the basic intention to act on what we have heard. Practical obedience hardly crosses the mind of those who merely want to *care for the spiritual side of life* by taking in an occasional church service or other religious event.

The concept of being yoked is a great corrective for our lack of context and intention. When Jesus invites us to share his yoke, he is calling us into his story, into the life-shaping orientation provided by his sense of *what the Father is doing*.

The passage from which the image and analogy of the yoke come is one of my very favorites. I can never think of the words *yoke, free, light* without simultaneously thinking of the time I first discovered them. It was the winter of 1978. Just out of business school at university, I was in my first term of Bible school in the mountains of Southern California. In a lecture on the Sermon on the Mount I first formed a vision for a life of light and easy obedience in Jesus. Jesus said, "Take my yoke upon you and learn from me, for I am gentle and humble in heart, and you will find rest for your souls" (Matthew 11:29 NIV).

This has been my favorite verse ever since. I am not sure why, but it grabbed my heart. For all of us who did not grow up around animals, I should say that a yoke is a wooden beam used between a pair of oxen to allow them to pull a load. I think

I loved the mental picture of being in a yoke with Jesus. The friends Debbie and I shared a home with while attending Bible school knew this and took a picture of a yoke on the side of a barn in West Virginia. Tim and Susie framed it nicely and placed a small bronze plate in the bottom of the frame with an inscription: "Stay in the Yoke . . . Matthew 11:29." In the years since, I have moved offices many times, but that picture has always hung prominently on the wall. A few years ago my wife, knowing my affection for the yoke image, bought an authentic yoke at an antique store and gave it to me as a Christmas present. It hangs in an important place on our porch.

As much as the yoke of Jesus has shaped my imagination for life in Jesus, its flame was fanned further the first time I read the same words in Matthew 11 of *The Message:*

> Are you tired? Worn out? Burned out on religion? Come to me. Get away with me and you'll recover your life. I'll show you how to take a real rest. Walk with me and work with me—watch how I do it. Learn the unforced rhythms of grace. I won't lay anything heavy or ill-fitting on you. *Keep company with me and you'll learn to live freely and lightly.* (emphasis added)

Judging from the context of this passage of Scripture, Jesus is reacting to the tension, confusion and rejection going on around him. The Pharisees were known to encourage people to wear the yoke of the Torah, the heavy burden of Jewish law. Jesus offered a new way of being faithful to God that was easy and light—straightforward and uncomplicated, not ponderous or harsh.

How does an "easy yoke" work with "the demands" of following Jesus, the things we have to change or leave behind? They are in play, but they are not enforced like a mean gym teacher who makes you run endless laps for a minor infraction of the rules. And, besides, what if those requirements are actually a part of what creates freedom and lightness of heart and spirit?

The load of following Jesus is not lighter because Jesus has a "Whatever!" mentality about morals, but because he carries most of the load. The Pharisees, on the other hand, laid heavy burdens on people and didn't lift a finger to help them. When we are yoked with Jesus, the *work* God wants done will happen in us and through us.

FREE AND LIGHT SPIRITUALITY

When Jesus uses the words *my yoke* he means to give us a vision for *the service of God as he teaches it*. The contrast is not between having and not having a yoke, but between *his teaching* (light yoke) and the *scribe's teaching* (heavy yoke). It is a modern bit of hubris and arrogant imagination to think that any of us can live with no yoke.

Everyone learns to do life from others. Some people follow Oprah, Dr. Phil, Keith Olbermann or Rush Limbaugh. Others follow a grandparent or loved teacher. I suppose any of these are okay as far as they might align with the story of God. But it is a delusion to think we can live without the yoke of a teacher who gives understanding about life. *We all make a radical choice: We choose our teacher, and then we take our instruction and training.*

Thus, we need to decide: In whose yoke do we want to live? Not only is Jesus' yoke free and light, the road he is walking is easy. The broad way leading to destruction is the hard road.

Just ask anyone who cannot get their life together because of addictions and other self-destructive behaviors. Jesus is not just our powerful Savior and Lord. He is actually *good*—and provides a good yoke and good road. We will never act on sermons until we believe this is true.

HEARING SERMONS WITHIN A FREE AND LIGHT LIFE

Okay, if a free and light life of following Jesus is available, how do we interact with sermons to move in that direction? I've been on both sides of mediocre sermons, a giver and a taker! Let's see if we can set aside normal worries and experiences with sermons—great, good or average—and focus instead on how we can repractice them as hearing God for the sake of entering the life Jesus calls us to.

To begin repracticing hearing sermons so they translate into a free and light life, we might want to start with the epistle of James. James says we betray something significant and make a big mistake when we "let the word go in one ear and out the other." He urges his readers to "act on what you hear." He said if we do we will "find delight and affirmation in the action" (James 1:22-25).

Many of us do not experience James to be right. Our experience tell us that practicing Christianity is hard. Let's look at two versions of Ephesians 5:3-4 as an example:

> But sexual immorality and all impurity or covetousness must not even be named among you, as is proper among saints. Let there be no filthiness nor foolish talk nor crude joking, which are out of place, but instead let there be thanksgiving. (ESV)

Don't allow love to turn into lust, setting off a downhill slide into sexual promiscuity, filthy practices, or bullying greed. Though some tongues just love the taste of gossip, those who follow Jesus have better uses for language than that. Don't talk dirty or silly. That kind of talk doesn't fit our style. Thanksgiving is our dialect.

I wonder if we don't hear a text like this and think, *Well I don't run a porn shop; I don't cuss people out or tell jokes that tear people down.* We when respond in this manner, we miss the point. We miss the opportunity to participate in Jesus' easy yoke. Paul is discussing that which is normal in God's new society. He's describing what naturally happens to those who share the yoke of Jesus. These are not *rules you have to obey* to keep yourself from burning in hell. Thinking of Paul's metaphor in Colossians 3:12, these are the new clothes we put on as we begin to follow Jesus.

As an illustration, let's talk about cussing. I've been asked in the past to take part in a debate about whether it's okay for Christians to use certain swear words. I found the whole thing very odd. I kept wondering why anyone would want to cuss. Some said that sometimes a swear word is perfect for the context. Others thought it was prudish to expect Christians to not occasionally drop the F-bomb or curse someone. This approach seriously misses the point for those who are trying to make their way while yoked to Jesus.

While words are undoubtedly important and powerful, I don't think Paul has mere words in mind. He is thinking of something more like *the nature of things* for those who are yoked with Jesus. The underlying sense of the Greek behind this sentence means there should be "no dirty minds among us expressing themselves in dirty words." When we pay closer attention to the inward reality—the mind from which words come—we move from a legalistic concern for which words we can use to the essential inner nature Paul has in mind. My basic contribution to the cussing debate is this: use the Golden Rule as your guide. If you don't like being cussed out, then don't do it to others. The Golden Rule is key to moving and operating in rhythm and alignment with Jesus.

THE NARROW WAY IS THE EASY WAY

Here is a surprising thought: Jesus said the narrow way of following him is the easy way. It is the path to life, not hardship and death. This is a self-authenticating truth—all we have to do is try it. Let me emphasize again: the wide path of not following Jesus is hard and destructive (Matthew 7:13-14). Just ask any recovering addict or someone with a besetting, life-harming sin.

Okay, if James is right, that in order to find life, hearing must be accompanied by doing, how does *doing* relate to having a *free and light* yoke? Jesus said those two things are joined by faith, which facilitates an ability to calm down and lighten up:

> What I'm trying to do here is get you to relax, not be so preoccupied with getting so you can respond to God's *giving*. People who don't know God and the way he works fuss over these things, but you know both God and how he works. Steep yourself in God-reality, God-initiative, God-provisions. You'll find all your everyday human concerns will be met. Don't be afraid of missing out. You're my dearest friends! The Father wants to give you the very kingdom itself. (Luke 12:29-32)

I value the connection in this passage between *relax* and *the way God works*. "Light" and "free" go out the window for me when I slip up and find myself out of the yoke—not staying connected to Jesus through the spiritual practice of hearing sermons. Often this is subconscious; I just get too busy, too preoccupied, too worried and anxious, and thus find that I am walking alone—outside the yoke. Someone told me a great definition of functional atheism: the thought or feeling that *nothing good is going to happen here unless I make it happen*. Though I am not an atheist, when I forget *how God works*, I sometimes function like one! But when I use the spiritual practice of hearing sermons to assist me with a pattern of steeping myself in "God-reality," "God-initiative" and "God-provisions," I find my way to a freer, less weighted-down life.

I am always displeased when I act in little-faith ways, knowing God says I am his *dearest friend* and he wants to give me the *kingdom itself.* God's provisions, friends, the kingdom itself, these are parallel to Jesus' free and light life when we are yoked with him. They should also remind us that though life can be hard, the intention of God and of true Christian spirituality is not to add to these hardships. Rather they are intended to strengthen us in trials and to make us the kind of people who can comfort others with the comfort we have received (2 Corinthians 1:4-7).

NOT ALL ROADS LEAD TO A FREE LIFE

Philip Yancey recounts a conversation he had with some leaders of *Pravda* (the Russian news organization) who were wondering aloud about "communism's fall from grace" and the parallel dramatic drop in circulation for *Pravda.* They "remarked wistfully that Christianity and communism have many of the same ideals: equality, sharing, justice, and racial harmony." "Yet," Yancey recounts, "they had to admit the Marxist pursuit of that vision had produced the worst nightmares the world has ever seen." These leaders sincerely wondered why this was so. "We [communists] do not know how to motivate people to show compassion. . . . [W]e tried raising money for the children of Chernobyl, but the average Russian citizen would rather spend his money on drink. How do you reform and motivate people? How do you get them to be good?"

This is an age-old question asked by parents and moral philosophers alike: how do we get someone to be good? One reply is to say that goodness is found only in a certain context—a story—the story of God. The Scriptures—both the Old and New Testaments—tell a story of creation and new creation. This theme comes through in millions of sermons every year. We need to repractice those sermons and so the biblical story becomes the means to a free and light life. We need to listen to and read the story to discover not only "the story so far" but also "how it is supposed to end." As we learn the overall story of the Bible,

> we must allow the power of God's promised future have its way with us. . . . We read it to discover the story of how God's kingdom was established on earth as in heaven in and through the work of Jesus, fulfilling Israel's great story, defeating the power of evil, and launching God's new world.

Once we know and become part of this story, as actors within it we can work our way, in real faith and confidence, to a set of

life values and life practices that emerge as the natural conse-
quence of being yoked with Jesus.

MISUSING SERMONS ON
EITHER SIDE OF THE PULPIT

Unfortunately, preachers sometimes *sermonize*, which means
they use a dogmatic, condescending, manipulative, guilt-
producing style of communication. Even if a preacher doesn't
mean it that way, those in the pews are conditioned to hear it in
that manner. Like millions of others, I loved *The Shack*. The following dialogue between Mack and the persons of the Trinity
show how misunderstandings of Christian spirituality easily
get in the way of a free and light life:

> *Mack says to Jesus:* Don't you want us to set priorities You
> know: God first, then whatever follows from whatever?
>
> *Sarayu (the Holy Spirit) answers:* The trouble with living
> by priorities . . . is that it sees everything as a hierarchy, a
> pyramid . . . and if you put God at the top, what does that
> really mean and how much is enough? How much time do
> you have to give me before you can go on about the rest of
> your day, the part that interests you so much more?
>
> *Papa (God the Father) interrupts:* You see, Mackenzie, I
> don't just want a piece of you and a piece of your life. Even
> if you were able, which you are not, to give me the biggest
> piece, that is not what I want. I want all of you and all of
> every part of you.
>
> *Jesus then speaks again:* Mack, I don't want to be first
> among a list of values; I want to be at the center of every-
> thing. When I live in you, then together we can live
> through everything that happens to you.

That passage is for me is a classic portrayal of both what can go wrong and what can go right as we repractice hearing sermons. Somehow we must reconfigure listening to sermons to mean taking on a new way of thinking about interacting with Jesus. We can never let our life with Jesus turn into a depersonalized set of principles. Being yoked with Jesus is a new way of living in a new story—the story of God. When we listen to sermons with this in mind, they become a key part of our spiritual formation.

Another difficulty with the spiritual practice of hearing sermons comes from thinking we know more than we actually do. This insight comes from Eugene Peterson. He describes what it is like for those of us who have taught the Bible for decades, engaged in spiritual counseling or had other highly visible roles in the church. This thought has crossed my mind many times:

> Who am I and what people think I am aren't anywhere close to being the same thing. The better I get as a [pastor] and the more my reputation grows, the more I feel like a fraud. I know so much more than I live. The longer I live, the more knowledge I acquire, the wider the gap between what I know and what I live. I'm getting worse by the day.

Maybe you can relate too. Maybe you don't have to be a church professional to fall into this trap. What is the way out? How do we repractice hearing sermons so that they produce *life* and not *guilt*? Here is a hint: "The work of the Spirit in creation is no longer confined to asking the questions 'When did this take place? How did this happen?' We are now asking 'How can I get in on this? Where is my place in this?' And praying, 'Create in me . . .' (Psalm 51:10)." I suggest we listen to sermons this way—no matter what the preacher is saying. For instance, suppose the preacher says, "Paul wrote this letter in the year XYZ, to ABC people to communicate to them D, E and F." As we listen we say to ourselves, *Wow! How can I get in on this? Where is my place in this? How do I embody this story in my life, my times, my people and the challenges of my world?* Now we're cookin'— we are repracticing sermons into a way of life.

SERMONS: FULFILLING THE MESSAGE

Here is another way to think about how sermons can be repracticed into a free and light life. Jesus' first presentation, his first *sermon*, announced that a new reality was breaking into the affairs of all humanity in and through him. Jesus called this reality the kingdom of God. This new kingdom—announced, embodied and demonstrated by Jesus—called for and enabled a new way of living, a new way of being human. Growing from a small seed to a large tree, the way of the kingdom would one day lead fallen people to become truly human as God intended. Thus, in Christian spirituality we move from a *message* to a *way*. And spiritual *practices* make possible the way, cooperating with and fulfilling the message.

Fulfilling the message is precisely what we are after as we envision moving from hearing sermons to a free and light life in Jesus. Sermons are instrumental; they are a means to being better yoked with Jesus. The freedom and light gained by being *yoked with Jesus* is the active ingredient for spiritual life, which gives hope to those wandering on the edges of faith, wondering: *Is there anything real in there?*

Free and light lives know the answer: Yes!

Following Liturgy

A Lifestyle of the Work of the People

"This is a large work I've called you into,
but don't be overwhelmed by it. It is best to start small."

MATTHEW 10:40

"There is far more at stake here than religion.
If you had any idea what this Scripture meant—'I prefer a flexible heart
to an inflexible ritual'—you wouldn't be nitpicking like this."

MATTHEW 12:6

I've had moments when I have been an equal-opportunity nit-
picker—I can cynically criticize both church and godly service.
Lately I've been engaging in the spiritual practice of liturgy
with the intent of doing the work of God's people outside the
church within the rhythms and routines of my daily life.

The United Methodist Church has a clear pattern for worship, but even though I grew up Methodist I am ashamed to say I did not pay enough attention to tell you what it is! Later, at Calvary Chapel, we too had a routine way of doing church: up-tempo Christian choruses, announcements and offering, a Bible-based sermon, an altar call, a closing song, and dismissal. Though no one said, "This is the right way to do church," we *knew* it was. It did not need to be explained or defended.

Nonliturgical, for most people, calls to mind worship that is not Catholic, Anglican, Lutheran or Orthodox. But every church has a liturgy—a way, a manner, a pattern or a prescribed order for public worship. The question is not *Do we have a liturgy?* but *Is our liturgy good and useful? Does it effectively produce worshiping and serving apprentices of Jesus?*

Upon hearing the word *liturgy*, most of us think of the prescribed order of a church service, the established forms of worship, including Scripture readings, prayers, creeds and so forth. This is not wrong. In some traditions, liturgy also includes the Christian calendar and daily offices. *Liturgy* comes from a Greek word that means "public work," "public duty" or "the work of the people." It can refer to a public good done by a person of wealth. The Greek New Testament borrowed the word to describe the work or "service" done by followers of Jesus. For instance, in Philippians 2:17, Paul encourages steadfastness in the faith among the church in Philippi by appealing to his "sacrifice" and "service." Only much later did *liturgy* come to mean "the prescribed service of Eucharist" in the limited way we think of it today. Paul envisioned his life as a sacrifice lived in public for the sake of others. This points us in the right direction to connect liturgy to life.

WORSHIP RECONSIDERED

Using liturgy as a launching pad, how can we engage in the spiritual practice of liturgy in a way that leads to the work of the people *outside* the four walls of a church building, in public space? I want to help shape our imagination around a crucial thought: *worship* stands for *a people and their lives*, not merely *a time and place* where certain religious things happen. The form we use is not central or ultimate in Christian worship. Form is merely the means or scaffolding that allows the real work to be done—public service to God by publicly serving others.

The biblical words used for *worship* provide clues for moving from liturgy thought of as *church* to liturgy as *a lifestyle.* One of the most common Hebrew words for worship comes from a root word that means *servant.* The most common New Testament word for "worship" (in Greek, *proskunc*) connects worship—*ascribing worth to God*—to public service *(latrev),* thus making Christian worship and service inseparable, like a loving mother with newborn baby. This enables liturgy to include acts of service of all kinds, in and out of church services. Worshiping God is not just singing, saying prayers, listening to a sermon, taking communion and giving offerings—though it includes these. Worship is equally *serving* God by pursuing our own spiritual transformation into Christlikeness in order to be his agents, his salt and light on the earth.

LITURGY AS VOCATION

Liturgy is the "work of the people." That means that our actual work in the world can become an aspect of our worship. Even though I know differently, when I hear the word *vocation,* my mind jumps to my *job,* or at least the job of someone who has some sort of *calling*—like a minister or a teacher or a nurse. But who would think of the lady at the local FedEx store or the guy picking up my trash or the person minding the parking meters as expressing their calling? This thinking can leave us in a terrible state. If we do not count the time and energy expended on our day-to-day work as our real calling or vocation, then we lose forty to sixty hours per week of fertile soil for our spiritual formation and a great opportunity to do the work of God's people.

This has not always been the case. Ancient church liturgies were designed to be used in everyday life. *Their purpose was not just to organize worship services but to shape lives.* The biblical words for worship, service and ministry are connected. This connection teaches us that all of life matters. Christians are called to be apprentices of Jesus; this is our vocation. By definition this covers all of life. Apprenticeship cannot be compartmentalized so that it excludes my career, my family and my hobbies.

Worship and devotion, if they are to lead naturally and easily to service and ministry, must begin by loving God enough to pay attention to him and his agenda in the *world*, not just on Sunday morning. This is one reason church signs and notice boards can be misleading: Worship: 10:00 a.m. Worship has too often been reduced to this one hour on Sunday rather than the worship hour being seen as a small but important component of an overall life of devotion to God and service to others.

In ancient Israel the people responded to God's grace and initiative through feasts and festivals at set times and places. A good deal of the first five books of our Bibles are given over to prescribing how these meetings should happen. Thus we can't say that having prescribed meetings at prearranged times in set places are wrong or bad or pointless. Here, the problem is not the thing itself—the people of God gathered for worship. The problem is a lack of context and a reductionistic tendency regarding worship. Let's examine these two errors that separate liturgy from a vocational lifestyle.

First, worship arises in and happens within a context. The highly informative, imagination-shaping context that points us to a whole-life understanding is our covenant with God. In the covenant, God promises to deliver, redeem and bless his people. But crucial to a holistic understanding of worship, in the covenant God also gives obligations to his people: a lifestyle marked by certain behavior (the Ten Commandments) and a lifestyle of blessing God through grateful worship and cheerful obedience. The new covenant through Jesus deepens, empowers (through the Holy Spirit) and makes all-inclusive (the Gentiles) the earlier covenant with Israel to live a life worthy of God's delivered, saved, Spirit-empowered people.

Think of the phrase we have heard a thousand times over the years: *Now we are going to move into a time of worship.* What were we doing before that announcement? What will we do after this "time of worship" is over? We either need new language or a fresh agreement that whatever such announcements mean, they do not signify that worship takes place only at certain times—as important and God-commanded as those times are. Worship needs to become "an orientation to life."

LITURGY: WORKING FROM YOUR HEART

In Colossians 3 Paul makes his customary turn from *what* to *so what*, from *theology* to *the life* that should naturally spring from what he has just written. This chapter is dominated by the idea that those who follow Jesus are to live in harmony with his victory over evil and the powers contrary to God. We are to "set [our] hearts on things above, where Christ is seated at the right hand of God" and to "set [our] minds on things above, not on earthly things" (Colossians 3:1-2 NIV). Paul then enumerates some practical life issues for reengaging the spiritual practice of liturgy in our everyday work:

> Servants, do what you're told by your earthly masters. And don't just do the minimum that will get you by. Do your best. Work from the heart for your real Master, for God, confident that you'll get paid in full when you come into your inheritance. Keep in mind always that the ultimate Master you're serving is Christ. The sullen servant who does shoddy work will be held responsible. Being a follower of Jesus doesn't cover up bad work. (Colossians 3:22-24)

Clearly Paul thinks that all ethical work is part of a holy and Spirit-filled life. He aims specifically to give dignity to even repetitive and menial work by dedicating it to God. Our work of worship empowers this manner work in society. The key idea is that liturgy should not just shape our thinking but *form our lives*. This is repracticing liturgy.

Form our lives? I don't think that thought would have crossed my mind twenty-five to thirty years ago. Thus the present renewal of interest in liturgy is interesting to me, not least because I am now serving in the Anglican Mission in the Americas. I have mostly known people who were tired of stale, dry, nonlife-transforming liturgy and were therefore flocking to Vineyard churches because of the outstanding worship music and healing presence of God.

However it is sad, even heartbreaking, that millions of people who fought in the worship wars of the last thirty-five years are now disillusioned with contemporary Christian worship. We now understand that the dualistic thinking that pitted *liturgical worship* against *contemporary worship* was wrong and unhelpful.

Using the Vineyard as an illustration, we certainly had a prescribed liturgy. We may not have fought over precise words like our liturgical forebears, but we had our own issues we were willing to quarrel about. The Vineyard liturgy went like this: (1) thirty minutes of uninterrupted singing (one of the biggest faux pas a worship leader could commit was to talk in the middle of "worship"), which began with a call-to-worship type song and progressed through a prescribed pattern to what we called *intimate* songs; (2) announcements; (3) teaching from the Bible; and (4) *ministry time*—that is, we prayed for the sick and so forth while singing a song or two.

None of this is bad or wrong. In fact I saw people transformed by it. But now some people are hungry and thirsty for liturgical worship, while others—thinking it dry, dull and rote—want nothing to do with it. Both styles can let people down. For instance, if liturgical worship is all that great, how do we explain the rampant apostasy in large swaths of the liturgical church world? On the other hand, how is it that evangelical churchgoers can listen to sermons for decades and still be immature, judgmental and sinful people?

For us liturgical types, we need to embrace the spiritual practice of liturgy so that liturgy becomes a practice for life. And the repracticing of liturgy will work in any setting: Baptist, Calvary Chapel, Presbyterian or Anglican churches. The repracticing of liturgy will then empower the patterns of worship in each, reforming not just words but also lives.

WITNESSING: LIVING A LITURGICAL LIFE

This brings into play a word we might not automatically link to liturgy, the work of the people: *witnessing*. There is probably no better place to witness than at work (and I don't mean leaving tracts in obvious places). A life rooted in worship is demonstrated in simple things like a good attitude, serving others, being patient in trials, working, as Paul said, "as unto God," not just for our boss.

A big problem with witnessing today is that it seems disconnected from real life. I recently saw a bumper sticker hollering "Focus on Your Own Damn Family!" I interpret this as saying, *Please stop sermonizing to us!* Though our words fail, living a genuine and humble life of faith in our daily routines—which for most adults is the workplace—is a great form of witness. It allows those outside the church to see that there is something going on in us besides our use of religious terms.

Being real (e.g., liturgy as the work of the people) is an effective means of witnessing today. Why? Today, not much seems substantive, reliable and durable. Words are fleeting. Commitment is passé. But when we repractice liturgy, living with compassion in service of others, we are witnessing to new life in Christ. There is indeed something real that proceeds from God as his people engage with him in worship.

LITURGY: THE WORK OF THE PEOPLE

In liturgical theology, belief and doctrine begin and end in worship and prayer. We might say that belief and doctrine end in worship understood as a lifestyle of service to God and others (the work of the people), and in prayer, conceived of as an ongoing conversational relationship with God. Liturgy does not provide merely a recognizable pattern for meetings of a congregation; it also tells us a scriptural story in which we find discernible patterns for being the people of God, repracticing liturgies of all kinds in order to do the work of the people as our *reasonable act of worship.*

The word translated *worship* in Romans 12:1 is literally *service.* The Amplified Bible says "service and worship"; Young's Literal Translation has "intelligent service"; the New American Standard Bible says "spiritual service of worship"; and several versions, including the New King James, translate it as "reasonable service." What do we make of this? These translations rightly tease from *latreia* (Greek for "service") ideas which shape our understanding of liturgy as a way life. They give us a vision for repracticing liturgy as service to God in the form of serving others as the work of the people of God.

LARGE WORK: START SMALL, BE FLEXIBLE

In the quote at the beginning of this chapter, Jesus calls his followers into the work of being God's people for the sake of others. Recently I had a firsthand look at how this calling makes good sense to church insiders *and* outsiders as well.

This past summer my son did some part-time work for me on his break from college. Getting ready to experience the empty-nest stage of life, I especially loved having him around. Jonathan is still exploring the exact nature of his faith, but working with me as we geared-up the "Three Is Enough" website, he got to see what Dad was up to. Three Is Enough gives people a simple and doable way of serving God and others in their everyday lives. I could see he was interested, so I asked him to write something from his own heart about what he saw going on, something we could put on the website for people like him. Here is what he wrote:

Hi, my name is Jonathan and I am Todd's son and I have just recently started working for 3isenough. Until just today I had no real knowledge of what 3isenough was or what my father was trying to accomplish. After reading the website and listening to the Twin Cities audio I have come to the conclusion for myself that it is all about "getting people to be people to each other."

I am not the most religious person in the world by far, but nonetheless this is how I have lived my life for twenty three years with the people in my life. Up until now I have never once thought of it as religious or Christlike; it's just the way I am. I strongly believe the world needs people to be "people" to each other. I see in my everyday life that people are too disconnected from each other and have too much apathy towards one another.

I also think that this is the best and most nonthreatening way for Christians and non-Christians alike to come together on a common goal that I believe most people in this world want: a better place to live. Like I said earlier, I have had no knowledge that this is what my father is trying to accomplish and to find out that we share a common goal or "thought" is pretty profound for me.

Is this entirely a coincidence that I have started working for my father? Or is it not. That I am not sure of myself. But I am sure that we are a perfect example of a reli-

gious person and a nonreligious person coming together
for this common goal.

People, being people to each other.

Liturgy is the public work of the people. So in this sense
church is public. It is a *sacred* entity within a larger *secular* reality. When we rightly engage in the spiritual practice of liturgy
in both church (private) and work (public), we discover what
both *churchy* people (me) and *nonchurchy* people (Jonathan)
know to be true: we draw equally close to God by providing for
orphans and widows as we do when we perform the liturgy in
church—both are the work of the people.

Giving an Offering

Simplicity of Life

"If a person gets his attitude toward money straight, it will help
straighten out almost every other area of his life."

BILLY GRAHAM

"Remember this—you can't serve God and money,
but you can serve God with money."

SELWYN HUGHES

"Make all you can . . . save all you can . . . give all you can."

JOHN WESLEY

Within the first few weeks of becoming a Christian, the person who led me to the Lord mentioned the word *tithing*. I didn't first hear the word in a desperate or manipulative sermon. It didn't come up in the middle of a building campaign. It came up naturally, sitting on stools around the island in our kitchen. I was twenty-one, not quite out of college. My wife and I have been tithing for the ensuing decades. Along the way I discovered there is a whole lifestyle of which tithing just scratches the surface.

If there is any Christian practice that needs to be repracticed these days, it is surely tithing. There is much controversy over whether tithing is a biblically commanded practice. Some less-than-generous Christians hope giving 10 percent is not required of "New Testament" believers—people like you and me.

The national average household income is approximately $50,000 per year. If we were to go to church forty times a year (most Christians don't go that often) and put twenty bucks in the offering plate each time, we'd be giving $800 per year—which is far less than 10 percent. But what if we also give $100 to the heart association and $100 to breast cancer research? Okay, now we're up to $1,000—still way below a tithe.

Over the years I've even heard long and loud arguments over whether we are supposed to tithe on our net pay or gross pay. Talk about missing the point! Pastors and church treasurers love the idea of tithing, and they *know* that it should go to the church first. But even if we come to the conclusion that tithing is not a biblically commanded practice for "the church age," money and giving are still really big topics in the Bible. This is why Billy Graham's quote—"If a person gets his attitude toward money straight, it will help straighten out almost every other area of his life"—is spot on.

In this chapter I am not going to engage in a thorough exploration of the biblical basis for tithing—or the lack of it. We have something more important to do. We all know Christians are to give, so on that basis, let's see if can move from perfunctory tithing formulas to see what engaging the spiritual practice of giving will produce.

GIVING AS A HABIT OF LIFE

Most tithing is done mechanically, out of obligation and with little thought, except for the occasional insight that *we could make payments for a new car with what we are giving to church every month!* While I don't regret that we give or wish we were spending it on ourselves, I am somewhat guilty of the mechanical part. As I said, Debbie and I have been practicing tithing (and more) for our entire married life. We have never gone without anything important. In fact, we have been uncommonly blessed. But I should hasten to say that we have never thought of this as a quid pro quo with God, a "tit for tat" or "you scratch my back and I'll scratch yours." It has become routine. In 90 percent of the approximately thousand paychecks I have received in my working life, giving 10 percent to the church was easy to do. Even if it had been hard, we still would have done it.

For Debbie, it is more personal, more grounded. She does all our bills and all our banking. While I always know my approximate annual income, most of time I could not even tell you how much my twice-a-month checks are or how much I have made from speaking, teaching and writing. Much of the time I do not even know how much we tithe or what we give to Compassion International, to missionaries, to friends in need and so on. I can't even name all the people and organizations we give to. But Debbie can. I short, for me, all the personal, relational and experiential aspects of giving have largely disappeared. I am only connected meaningfully to *the other* or to *the least of these* on the occasions I write a letter to the children we support through Compassion, or when a friend or family member needs immediate and vital help—the kind of thing Debbie and I would be apt to talk about.

I never planned to go down this road. I think our giving routine started positively as an acknowledgment that everything we have belongs to God. But somehow all the particularity vanished, for me. And when particularity is gone from my spiritual life, something crucial is missing. How can we have Christlike compassion when particularity is gone? What is compassion if it is not personal. Jesus was not a principle or a theory. He was grounded in real flesh, actual people and authentic doings of life. Our spirituality, our practices and in this case our giving only work in concert with God when it is personal—between us and God and between us and those we concretely love through our giving.

I guess someone could say that my little confession is not all bad; after all, it betrays the good habit of giving to others. But here is my self-criticism: I think the habit, though a good one, is more rooted in requirement and responsibility than in a deep and personal care for *the other*. This is why I want to repractice tithing in my own life, and why I commend these thoughts to you. I want you to do a giving inventory: how much, to whom, why, how do you feel about it, how closely connected is your giving to God and to others?

I think I may have come up with an answer for myself. I think I may have been practicing giving without the corresponding practice of simplicity. For help in simplicity I turn back to where I started the journey of reengaging the spiritual practices of church. I think back to 1991 and to my beloved friend and guide Richard Foster.

SIMPLICITY IS FREEDOM

In his model book *Celebration of Discipline*, Richard teaches us that *simplicity* is freedom; *duplicity* is bondage. Richard chooses words better than anyone I know. He is a very careful writer—so much so that we often miss the depth of what he is teaching if we do not pause to unpack his thoughts, which I'll expand on here.

- *Simplicity* is the state of being uncombined, uncomplicated or uncompounded; it is freedom from pretense.

- *Freedom* is free will, independence and autonomy; but it is not just absence of restraints, or frustration from being short of liberty, it is also the capacity to act. Freedom is for something; that is, Israel is set free from oppression in a foreign land *to be* the salt and light people of God.

- *Duplicity* moves in the direction of complexity; it is contradictory, at odds, incongruous and inconsistent with other held or stated values, priorities, ideals and principles.

- *Bondage* is to be enslaved by either a higher power or to be bound by a powerful inner compulsion, such as *bondage to buying and having*, etc.

Richard completes his thought on simplicity with "*Simplicity* brings freedom and joy. *Duplicity* brings anxiety and fear." As I respond to Richard's thoughts, I am not just thinking about tithing or giving but about the totality of my life. I think my biggest besetting issues are—and Debbie, Jonathan and Carol would probably agree with me—*sinful perfectionism* and the anxiety, fear and pride that flows from it. My sporadic tight neck and shoulders, my sometimes tight lower back and the occasional bouts with my jaws (TMJ) and associated pain in my teeth, head and the like show this is true.

I think I've discovered why tithing has never produced the freedom, joy and transformation I suppose it should: I give, but I have kept up my *duplicity*. Actually in my case it was worse—I kept up my *multiplicity*. I've always wanted or felt that I needed multiples of things to be happy and content. I clearly see what Foster means when he says, "Compulsive extravagance is a modern mania. The contemporary lust for 'more, more, more' is clearly psychotic; it has completely lost touch with reality."

I have discovered that lots of us need to repractice our faith by tithing with grace and with an intelligent, but not legalistic or neurotic, examination of what the practice is doing to our faith and what it might be doing to others.

For instance, digging deeper into Foster, we learn "the sheer fact that a person is living without things is not a guarantee that he or she is living in simplicity. . . . It is possible to develop an outward life-style of simplicity and to be filled with anxiety." This is true because it is the *love* of things and money that are at the root of the evil in duplicity and bondage. Any time we are talking about repracticing Christianity, our heart is in view. That's what I think went wrong with my giving: my heart got disconnected from my checkbook practices. In giving, tithing and simplicity, we are saying *no* to some things so that we can say *yes* to others. It is the *yes* that makes life whole, binding heart and hand, transforming us as we go.

The thing about money, Foster taught me, is that it cannot be seen as merely a disinterested object used for commerce. Rather, it has character to it, a power. Money in my view is an example of what Paul calls "principalities and powers." We need a new practice in order to break free from these powers and move from giving to simplicity—having Jesus' attitude toward both money and *the least of these*. The historic Christian view of money is: Get it and use it. But use it in Spirit-led, kingdom-based ways to love and serve others. Foster rightly says that it is a high calling—and counterintuitive and complex in my view—to use Mammon without serving Mammon.

As I seek to move from tithing to simplicity of life, I have taken up several Fosteresque challenges:

- to have a unified heart and singleness of purpose about my life—then money naturally falls into the proper pattern

- to learn contentment; I don't always need options and plurals

- to be delivered from covetousness, and to trust that I am always safe in the kingdom of God no matter what I have

- to be modest when it seems that only the loud and dominant get any attention today

- to receive what I have with gratitude, to rejoice in the goodness of God in ways that others will experience as for their good

- to find in simplicity a freedom that makes me lovingly available to others

- to develop the intellectual, emotional and relational energy, which is stored up by not neurotically pursuing more things

- to repractice my giving so that I move from mechanical obedience to joy and generosity

ROBBING GOD

This chapter on tithing would not be complete without looking at the famous passage on money and giving from Malachi 3:8: "Will a man rob God? Yet you rob me" (NIV). Let's start with the obvious: We can't take anything from God. Imagine God saying, "Rats! I knew I shouldn't have turned my back on those humans for even one second. I do and they take my iPod loaded with all my favorite songs and sermons!" "Robbing God" is a metaphor.

God is robbed (deprived or let down or rightly disappointed) when we fail to act in harmony with his intentions for humans. So when ancient Israel neglected God and failed to take care of the priests and the poor, they were robbing God, not by taking something from him but by failing to give him their devotion and loyalty, obedience and respect in keeping with their vocation as his people (see Genesis 12:1-3).

Actually, the aspect of the text that has always interested me more is the promise that follows the bit about robbing God.

> "Test me in this," says the LORD Almighty, "and see if I will not throw open the floodgates of heaven and pour out so much blessing that you will not have room enough for it. I will prevent pests from devouring your crops, and the vines in your fields will not cast their fruit," says the LORD Almighty. "Then all the nations will call you blessed, for yours will be a delightful land," says the LORD Almighty. (Malachi 3:10-12 NIV)

Clearly God has always intended to provide for his servants—his sent people; this is the essence of the promise. God is a huge advocate for the poor and the priests who serve him well. Don't take care of them, God says, and you are robbing me; take care of them on the other hand and see the blessing that will come to your lives!

I can hear some impatient readers wondering: When are you going to tell us if tithing is biblical and whether it should be on the gross or the net? Honestly, I don't have much new to add to the discussion. However, I don't think tithing is commanded for the Christ-redeemed, Spirit-created and empowered church. But this does not mean our giving should be something less than a tithe. I believe, and Debbie and I have lived as if, the New Testament requirement for generosity to God and others goes much further than the Old Testament requirement for a tithe.

The Old Testament tithe was very close to the taxes we pay today for our large social programs. In my decades of pastoring I've had many people in the church say to me, I already pay 35 percent (or whatever) in taxes for programs similar to what the Old Testament law required, so why do I have to give more to the church? I've always understood the basic logic behind this question, but what troubles me is the underlying motivation— to give as little as possible. That seems to me to be completely contrary to the whole spirit of the New Testament.

If I am right, those who follow Christ today are motivated and guided in giving by the indwelling Holy Spirit. But this does not let us off the hook. I fear that it could mean something closer to "sell all you have and give to the poor." Let me put my money where my mouth is: I pay tens of thousands of dollars in taxes every year. And while I do not agree with all the ways the government spends it, I do rejoice that the poor are being helped by my taxes. In addition Debbie and I give approximately—we are not legalistic about it—ten percent of our gross income to the church. On top of that we give to Compassion International, to friends in need and so on. And we have never lacked anything! In fact we have had so much that I have not done well, as I said earlier, with allowing the spiritual practice of giving to lead me into a simpler life.

What would happen if we shelved the various proof texts used in the tithing war and stepped back to ask how our conception of Christian giving would change if we read the Bible as story? What do you suppose is the trajectory of giving in the Bible? Is it stingy, grudging and resentful? Is it rightly used to magically get something from God? Or is it generous and others-oriented, mimicking the sacrificial life of Jesus? This is a pretty easy question to answer, and we don't even have to look for a proof text. I want to repractice tithing in this manner. We need to trust this instinct. It is the Holy Spirit teaching and leading us into all truth (John 16:13).

This Spirit-led giving is what Paul was getting at when he wrote: "Each man should give what he has decided in his heart to give, not reluctantly or under compulsion, for God loves a cheerful giver" (2 Corinthians 9:7 NIV). Luke, quoting Jesus, gives us the ground for Paul's thought by saying, "Give away your life; you'll find life given back, but not merely given back—given back with bonus and blessing. Giving, not getting, is the way. Generosity begets generosity" (Luke 6:38).

The spiritual practice of generosity, which comes from simplicity of heart, moves us from mere legalisms, compassionless mechanisms or stingy mathematical formulas of tithing to an ever simpler life for the sake of others.

8

Taking Communion

A Life of Thankfulness

"What happens in the Eucharist is that through the death
and resurrection of Jesus Christ, [the] future dimension is
brought sharply into play. . . . [W]e must see [the Eucharist]
as the arrival of God's future into the present, not just the
extension of God's past (or Jesus's past) into our present."

N. T. WRIGHT

Though I have been a minister for thirty years, I am a rookie
Anglican priest. A rookie is a novice or a recruit. I am a novice
recruited by God into the Anglican Mission. And boy do I feel
it, especially when it comes to leading communion. This past
winter, just after being ordained to the deaconate, I was asked
to assist with the Eucharist at a large conference of peers. The
gentleman who asked me to participate must have been shocked
when I responded, "No way. I might mess something up!" He

just smiled and walked away, maybe thinking, *They don't make deacons like they used to!*

But it gets worse! I've spoken to small, medium and large groups of people throughout my life, and I almost never get nervous. But the first few times I had to help with the Eucharist, I could barely put a handful of words together: "the body of Christ," "the bread of heaven" or "the blood of Christ, the cup of salvation." I'm not kidding; I stumbled over the words more often than I clearly enunciated them. And if someone responded with an appropriate "Amen," it startled me into a stuttering mess!

Clearly the Eucharist is indescribably significant. As a new priest, I hope I never get so comfortable with it that I lose being awed by its meaning and power. Not all of us come from the same church backgrounds, so I am going to pause a moment to reflect on what Communion is and why it is a spiritual practice that is so historically central to all followers of Jesus.

Our word *Eucharist*, sometimes called the Lord's Supper or Communion, comes from a Greek New Testament word meaning *thanksgiving* or *giving thanks*. The thanks involved here is twofold: Christ gave thanks at the meal which instituted the Eucharist, and the church throughout the ages has practiced the Eucharist as the supreme act of Christian thanksgiving. In this chapter we will discover how to engage the spiritual practice of Communion such that it imparts life to us. The "thanksgiving" is completed when the life we receive overflows to others—and they then give thanks for us, for the good they receive from us.

The Eucharist conveys to those who receive it in faith, the body and blood of Jesus, that is, Christ's life. It transmits by faith all the benefits of his broken body and shed blood, these being sacramental signs of the totality of his virgin birth, life, teachings, works, death, resurrection and ascension. No matter how we might explain it, the Eucharist is meant to be a real continuation of the life of Christ, just as the Passover was a continuation of God's deliverance from Egypt for the Jews.

The totality of Jesus' life and the meal he instituted are escha-tological events. In Jesus, and now in his meal, the perfected *end* of God is inaugurated in our present. This means that in the celebration of the Eucharist we partake of not just the life and death of Jesus. We also partake of the presence of the future; we receive life from Jesus' current life, the first fruits of the life to come. We receive the wholeness of this future life, inaugurated in us because of the death and resurrection of Jesus and the coming of the Spirit, as we celebrate the Eucharist. Though "es-chatology" may not be a new concept for most of us, it might be new in relation to Jesus' meal. Realizing that in Communion we partake of both the past and the future is the key to repracticing the Eucharist. Doing so provides the vision and power to live in such a manner that others will give thanks for us.

Through participating in the Eucharist we are announcing solidarity with the notion that God's new world has already bro-ken into this world. N. T. Wright says this would be laughable

> if it wasn't happening. But if a church is . . . actively in-volved in seeking justice in the world, both globally and locally, and if it's cheerfully celebrating God's good cre-ation and rescue from corruption in art and music, and if, in addition, its own internal life gives every sign that new creation is indeed happening, generating a new type of community—then suddenly the announcement makes a lot of sense.

SACRIFICE: THE HEART OF AN
OTHERS-ORIENTED LIFE

Let's look at the inner logic of the Eucharistic meal. In the Upper Room, Jesus gave thanks as he passed the broken bread and the cup among his first apprentices. As we receive what Jesus "passed," we feed on his life. We too, then, give thanks for the bread and wine we partake of today. As we participate in the Eucharist, our lives are transformed. Others experience our transformation as for their own good. When this sequence occurs, we are fully in line with the inner logic of holy Communion.

Nearly every pre-Reformation follower of Jesus would have instinctually understood the connection between participation in the Eucharist and a life of holiness and service to others. The same could be said of many Protestant and Catholic leaders after the Reformation. While they may have debated the exact nature of the Lord's Supper, they would have known the same reality: bread and wine taken in faith and obedience to Jesus leads to a transformed and transforming life.

This is also true today. The majority of our most admired Christian leaders are animated, energized and empowered by the reality of the eucharistic life, which directs them to seek justice and rescue others through life in the kingdom with Jesus.

Sacrifice is integral to the Eucharist. Through Christ's sacrifice and present-day intercession at the right hand of God, we receive new life and the power to live it. When our new life is expressed in Spirit-led sacrifice, others will give thanks for us even as we give thanks for Christ. Jesus did not distribute the bread and wine so we might adore them, but that they would be consumed. *Eat* and *drink* are action words, words of participation, and not just for church services but for living with Jesus and others daily.

Life is imparted *at* or *during* the Eucharist. Life is imparted
to the people and events of daily life through Eucharist-receiving
Christians. Thus in Communion we not only give thanks and
receive the power of Christ, we then live as he lived (as if he
were in our place), which in turns leads *others* to give thanks
for our lives. Historians and commentators of the first century
point out that this was the reputation of the early Christians.
As with the early followers of Jesus, his life is imparted to us,
and our lives infused with him are then lived for others. That
is a very simple connection. We do not need to be a theologian
to grasp this. Though it is simple, it is profound. In fact, it
could represent the whole of the story of God—his intention to
have a people who are his cooperative friends for the sake of
others.

Another way to look at this is that the imparted life Christians receive from Christ in Communion does not stop there—
or at least it shouldn't. I can imagine someone not actually par-
taking of Christ at the Eucharist because *their heart is not in it*,
but that is another matter. Real union with Christ doesn't stop
as we drive out of the church parking lot.

Focusing on *others* is the core idea. Others are at the heart of
our trinitarian God. We would have no knowledge of God if
this were not true. God created *others*—the first humans. He
did so that they would work alongside him. God called Abraham and made his family into Israel for the sake of the Gentiles. God sent the Spirit and created the church to serve the
rest of the world. In the bread and wine, we feast on Christ so
that others might partake of our fullness. The Eucharist does
not make us spiritual. We are spiritual by design. Receiving the

Eucharist empowers the already-existing Christ life within us, making us life-giving Christians—little Christs—in and for the world.

THE EUCHARIST DOES NOT WORK FOR ME

Someone may be thinking, *This is not what I have experienced in Communion, and I have been taking it since I was a kid. I hoped going to church and taking Communion would help me stop smoking, but it didn't, much less help me live a life others give thanks for!* Fair enough. Lots of people have gone to Communion and have continued to live ungodly lives of various sorts. So let's take a fearless and honest look at it. I feel no need to be (and I don't think any of us should be) defensive about Jesus, his meal or the church as it has practiced the Lord's Supper over the years. But clearly millions of people have not experienced the power and presence of Christ in Communion.

Communion is called a *sacrament*. Sacraments are historically and commonly defined as a visible form of an invisible grace, or the sign of a sacred reality. In the Eucharist, bread and wine are visible forms of the blessing received in them through Jesus who gave us this spiritual meal to practice. This sacramental relationship breaks down, however, if in our hearts and imaginations the Eucharist becomes a transaction with the church. Instead of Communion being connected to us personally, in the minds of many it is connected to church. Let's see if we can see why.

I don't think the essential problem is priests, ministers or the church. I think it is us. But not in the way many would think. I don't think all of us are taking Communion unworthily. The Eucharist doesn't lose its essential power because we keep on smoking (or whatever) even though we promised to stop through the power of the Eucharist. In cases like this, people often view the Eucharist as magic, which is superstition, not faith. We eat and drink, and then live by faith, not magic.

While mistaken views of the Eucharist are a real issue, in my experience they are not the main issue. I think the real culprit is that many of us have lost the context and story of the Eucharist—a loss so great that it keeps the Lord's Supper from touching the story of our lives.

Jesus didn't come on the scene out of nowhere; he arose within a particular story—the story of God creating a people through the life, death and resurrection of Jesus. These people were to be ambassadors of God, proclaiming, demonstrating and embodying his agenda—the kingdom—on earth. Similarly, the church did not arise out of the blue either. The Eucharist too takes place within a large, all-encompassing story, and not just the holy part of a church service or prescribed liturgy.

For the spiritual practice of Eucharist to enable Spirit-filled lives for which others naturally give thanks, we need the big picture of God's story. Out of his love, the triune God purposed to have cooperative friends on earth, so he created colaborers, Adam and Eve and their offspring. But they fell into sin and were separated from God. So God called Abraham and raised up and delivered Israel that God's name might be proclaimed throughout the earth. But because of their disobedience, God sent Israel into exile and delivered them once again. The story then moves to God's redemption, reconciliation and regeneration through the broken body and shed blood of Jesus. After Jesus' resurrection and ascension, God sent the Spirit and created the church, which is God's reconstituted friends who will labor with him according to his precreation intention. Finally, and still in the future, the story will reach its perfect conclusion in the renewed heaven and earth.

N. T. Wright is helpful here: "Within the sacramental world, past and present are one. Together they point forward to the still-future." Only within this comprehensive story of God does the Eucharist make its most enlivening, life-changing, Christ-partaking sense. Receiving the Eucharist without faith shaped by this story leaves us untouched. We remain bound in stories like "Why can't I quit smoking (or watching raunchy stuff, etc.) that destroys my soul?" The answer: "Without the Eucharist [participated in as a spiritual practice] it is very easy to drift into a spirituality that is dominated by ideas *about* Jesus instead of receiving life *from* Jesus." The Eucharist leads to the Christ life; Christlike life always leads others to naturally give thanks.

DO THIS IN REMEMBRANCE OF ME

Perhaps the following will make concrete what I am trying to say about the Eucharist.

First, a bit of background. I know that Jesus used the words "Do this in remembrance of me" with reference to the bread and wine he shared with his first followers. But in an effort to connect the spiritual practice of the Eucharist with the people and events of my life, I am wondering if Jesus' "do this" might also point me to another aspect of the Upper Room scene: the dirty towel lying by the washbasin of water dirtied from the disciples' feet.

Let's remind ourselves of the story from the Upper Room:

Jesus knew that the Father had put him in complete charge
of everything, that he came from God and was on his way

back to God. So he got up from the supper table, set aside his robe, and put on an apron. Then he poured water into a basin and began to wash the feet of the disciples, drying them with his apron. . . .

After he had finished washing their feet, he took his robe, put it back on, and went back to his place at the table.

Then he said, "Do you understand what I have done to you? You address me as 'Teacher' and 'Master,' and rightly so. That is what I am. So if I, the Master and Teacher, washed your feet, you must now wash each other's feet. I've laid down a pattern for you. What I've done, you do. . . . If you understand what I'm telling you, act like it—and live a blessed life." (John 13:3-5, 12-15, 17)

While the Eucharist rightly stands out in brilliant light, there was more going on in the Upper Room than just the special meal. If we are going to engage the spiritual practice of the Eucharist for the sake of others, we need to include the whole scene. For worship that leads to service, we need the chalice and broken bread *and* the towel of Jesus. The body and blood of Jesus represent more than his death on the cross. They signify everything that made his death effectual and worthy as a sacrifice: his matchless life of love, service and obedience to his Father.

Together the towel and meal show us how to participate in the spiritual practice of the Eucharist so that we take on the desire, power and means to live the Christlike life. Let's examine the Upper Room scene in more detail to see how this works.

Jesus knew that the Father had put him in complete charge of everything, that he came from God and was on his way back to God. Jesus was operating from an unseen Reality. That's right:

Reality with a capital *R*. He knew there was Reality behind *reality*. He wasn't stupid or floating through life as a mystical zombie. He was fully alert and fully alive. He knew he was in trouble with the authorities and that various groups were intent on harming him. He knew death was not far away. But he knew he was always safe in the plan and love of the Father—even in death! This is why he later told Peter to put away his sword—Jesus was safe; he could have called on legions of angels. He acted on the basis of his prior and all-grounding knowledge of who he was and where he came from.

He got up from the supper table, set aside his robe, and put on an apron. Then he poured water into a basin and began to wash the feet of the disciples. The motive for living for the sake of others is not primarily social, not even primarily about *social justice*. Nor is it moral. Serving as the friends of God and Jesus comes from a deep knowledge of God's love and purposes for us. Jesus, knowing this was true, wanted to impress this truth on the minds of his apprentices.

Do you understand what I have done to you? . . . If I, the Master and Teacher, washed your feet, you must now wash each other's feet. I've laid down a pattern for you. This pattern was not just for the Twelve but for all God's redeemed, Spirit-enlivened people. Jesus revealed (1) what all his followers are to do, (2) the humble, gentle and generous spirit from which they are to do it, and (3) the means for doing so: their ongoing character formation through God's power in the Eucharist. Jesus then lets them in on a big secret of life.

If you understand what I'm telling you, act like it—and live a blessed life. Receiving God's means of grace—the Eucharist and the filling of the Spirit—leads to spiritual life for the sake of others. The good life, the blessed life, is found in living as God's sent people. There is no greater invitation than the one to follow Jesus, to live as God's sent people for the sake of others.

We repractice the Lord's Supper well when we move from Eucharist as a *noun* to Eucharist as a *verb*. We participate in and receive the life of Christ in the Eucharist. The power of Jesus' life then flings us into a new life. We repractice the Eucharist well when we move from the passive reception of the *elements* to active, Jesus-filled, thanksgiving-expressing, Spirit-empowered use of Jesus' towel on behalf of the least, the last and the suffering.

GO IN PEACE TO LOVE AND SERVE THE LORD

The Book of Common Prayer has several dismissal prayers to use at the close of the Eucharist. The one we plan to use most at Holy Trinity Church in Costa Mesa, California, is "Go in peace to love and serve the Lord." As we say this week in and week out, we are shaping in ourselves a sent, missional worldview. In so doing we demonstrate our solidarity with God's broken world and our unity with the purpose of God for his people. As N. T. Wright says,

> [God] did not want to rescue humans *from* creation any more than he wanted to rescue Israel *from* the Gentiles. He wanted to rescue Israel *in order that Israel might be a light to the Gentiles*, and he wanted thereby to rescue humans *in order that humans might be his rescuing stewards over creation*. That is the inner dynamic of the kingdom of God.

That is also the inner dynamic of the spiritual practice of holy Communion done for the sake of others.

Receiving the Benediction

Blessing Others

"God's coming judgment is a good thing, something to be celebrated, longed for, yearned over. In a world of systematic injustice, bullying, violence, arrogance, and oppression, the thought that there might come a day when the wicked are firmly put in their place and the poor and weak are given their due is the best news there can be."

N. T. WRIGHT

Benedictions call to mind the end of an official religious event. I am sure that for many people, the word *benediction* reflexively brings forth "Thank God, church is almost over!" Most of us picture clergy in the front of the church lifting arms and speaking in a holy tone. In this chapter we will consider how we can repractice benedictions so that the blessing goes out the door with us—for the sake of others.

How *do* we leave our church's worship service? That is, in what inward posture do we leave church? In what frame of mind and heart? Do we leave thinking *I understand* or *I'm convinced?* The late Robert Webber said that at one point in his life "Christianity was no longer a power to be experienced but a system to be defended. [And] the more certain I became about my ability to defend God's existence and explain his character, the less real he seemed to me." Something more profound can happen than filling our intellect with information. Let's see if we can find a way to connect the spiritual practice of benediction such that it is both a blessing to be received and to pass on to others.

A benediction is a formal blessing that normally is the authoritative and official close to a Christian meeting. *Benediction* comes from a Latin word that means "to speak well." It is an invocation of divine presence and guidance, and the proclamation of God's favor on his people as they disperse. Many biblical passages are used as benedictions. The most famous of these blessings is the Aaronic Blessing found in the book of Numbers, which we will look at shortly. But first I'd like to consider a question.

How can knowledge and certainty, as Webber describes, be a barrier to experiencing divine reality? God certainly doesn't get angry when we think. The Bible is full of occasions when God implored his people to think well. Reading between Webber's lines I see something revealing in the way he contrasts power and experience with defending a system. Mere thought is useful in defending something. But experiencing power transcends mere *thinking*. Recall for a moment the well-known words of James 2:19: "You believe that there is one God. Good! Even the demons believe that—and shudder" (NIV). Believing (or thinking), as vital as it is, can and often does leave us hungry for the reality and power of experience.

There are many legitimate and truly helpful growth-producing ways to experience the power of God. But somewhere right near the top is working with Jesus, through the power of the Holy Spirit, to lead others to faith, heal the sick, relieve suffering and free the oppressed. In this tradition, Webber began a conversation that cleared an old path that seemed new to late-twentieth-century evangelicals. He explained the power of liturgical elements of worship and showed how they could work well with solid Bible teaching that told the story of God. Webber then added a crucial third leg: a life of serving real human needs, as Jesus did.

Most Protestants look back to the Reformation as their theological touchstone. But we often wrongly think that the Reformation was only about doctrine, primarily justification by faith through grace.

Actually, the Reformers were looking for a new kind of Christian life. They were disappointed by much of medieval spirituality and church life. They were looking for a version of the gospel that would produce sincere holiness and be a blessing to every village. Speaking of the English reformation, historian Stephen Neill explains, "They were convinced that the new understanding of the Gospel, with its appeal to the whole man, mind, and conscience and will, could bring about that inner reformation that to them was more important than any change in ritual or in the organization of the church." The Reformers were looking for a change that benefited others. They thought that Christians had one vocation, to be a saint for the sake of serving others.

The layman also is called to be a saint. [T]he place in which he must work out his saintliness is the home, the bank, the factory, the dock, the field, . . . and if he has understood his vocation, he can be sure that God will be as much with him there and he is with the priest saying [the benediction] in church.

I've known for quite some time that I needed to intensify and broaden my capacity to be blessed and to be a blessing to others. Most people who know me would say, "Oh, Todd, you've been kind and generous to me." I have no self-flagellating need to disagree, but the vast majority of these appraisers are from my social class. However, concerning people who are profoundly different from me—the sick, poor and the really annoying—I did not have the same ability to connect in helping and healing ways.

For instance, in hospitals I get unnervingly queasy when I see someone really ill or in severe pain. Interestingly, I have a very high tolerance for my own pain, but seeing others in pain literally makes me sick. At those moments I am usually way more attuned to the creepy feelings in my body than I am to the presence of God! And seeing God in annoying people? Well, I have to admit that I've got some spiritual growing to do.

For years I have heard that our heroes in the faith who work with the truly impoverished are themselves nourished by seeing Jesus in the faces of the poor. I have to admit I don't usually see Jesus' face in the poor. However, I have seen Jesus in someone who serves the poor.

The past few months our church in Boise has been feeding a hundred homeless people every week. My wife and a couple of others take turns cooking, and a few of us serve the meals and hang out with the women, children and men living on the street. Our participation was spurred on by Denie, a woman we met through a mutual friend. When we are with the homeless I see Jesus in the eyes of Denie. She knows most of the people by name; she gives them all big hugs and tells them that she loves them. While I am always happy to serve food and have light conversation, I am aware that Denie has something I just don't have. I need more work with the spiritual practice of benediction, more work with receiving and giving blessing.

LOVE IS THE MEASURE

Recently I related my self-appraisal to a group of friends. One of the young university students suggested I might be inspired by Dorothy Day. He even loaned me Day's biography, *Love Is the Measure*, to read. Dorothy Day is the founder of the Catholic Worker Movement, a somewhat controversial social-justice movement in the twentieth century.

I found Day simultaneously troubling, exciting, scary and a model worth imitating. She often said that her "awareness of the world's castoff people haunted her." It reminds me of a scene in the movie *Amazing Grace*—the story of William Wilberforce's work to abolish the slave trade in the United Kingdom. Wilberforce's former priest, John Newton, the author of the famous hymn "Amazing Grace," says that he (Newton) is haunted by the thousands of slaves he captured, tortured and sold or allowed to die. I can feel a similar "haunting" happening to me—haunting in the sense that I have a new awareness of the inequities of our new global reality.

A big part of what I'll never forget after reading about Day is how closely she identified with people who profoundly scare me. Not in the sense that I think a beggar is going to punch me or push a shopping cart into me (though I am sure it has happened to others!). Those kinds of scares and bruises heal fairly easily. I think my bigger, more profound fear is that intense poverty, severe disease and major social injustices could "take my life" if I ever took being an advocate on their behalf seriously. It's the difference a good country breakfast makes to a chicken and a pig: the eggs were just a contribution, but the bacon was a complete sacrifice!

I never have been able to imagine how people like Dorothy Day sacrifice everything yet say that they find life, real life, in so doing. Until I read Day's story I used to excuse myself by mumbling in my head something like, *Well, I just identify too strongly with pain; dealing with this level of hurt, poverty and injustice must not be my calling.* My other standby excuse: in the guise of helping others, many of the politicians I have known are actually creating power or enriching themselves. I've seen religious leaders do the same. But in Dorothy Day, Mother Teresa and many others, we see people who don't seek the spotlight, are completely altruistic and are selfless in an astonishing Christlike way.

Day often spent time in jail to act in solidarity with those suffering injustice and "to visit Jesus there," as the Gospels say. I am claustrophobic and couldn't spend one minute in a jail cell! After one ten-week period I had to quit an Alpha course I was helping to run in the local prison because I could not stand all the doors closing and locking behind me, reminding me that the guys with guns, keys and badges were in control, not me!

Startled by Day's story, I now think my excuses might be full of baloney! Finding Jesus in the kind of people she found him in will require that I embark on a new journey of spiritual transformation. Presently, I am looking for better insight by finding small ways to be more open to the outcasts of the world. Day moved from being an empathetic news reporter to a deeply involved caregiver and advocate. I hope I am on a similar trail—repracticing the blessing of benediction to become a blessing to others.

EMPOWERING A BLESSED AND BLESSING LIFE

A couple of things from Dorothy Day's story will never be far from my mind. First, she insisted that we see Jesus in the poor, the marginalized, the weak, the wounded, the least, the last and the lost. When Day was lonely, she found healing by walking the slums of New York City. This is important, but it may be difficult for those of us who tend to see Jesus in beautiful music, touching testimonies and well-crafted sermons. Those church-based things are not wrong or bad. In fact, the whole premise of this book is that they are good—especially so when they are a springboard to a new kind of life.

Second, Day was clear about the power of repracticing church elements in ways that were good for the poor. She emphasized that common church practices like early morning, daytime and evening prayer; celebrating Mass; silent retreats; and the advice of a spiritual director enabled her amazing, self-sacrificial life. Through my many years as a Christian I have rarely seen people making the connection that common religious practices lead to care for the poor. People these days are often devoted to such things as whales, trees, human sexuality and tolerance, but the spiritual practices of church, which today are held in low esteem, enlivened and sustained Day. While self-derived forms of service are all the rage, the practices of the church are passé.

Perhaps this disconnect explains why service is not deeper and more profound today. I wonder if contemporary forms of service can be sustained or be good for us and others without God's empowering presence through the normal means of grace—the church practices Day extolled. She said she could not do what she did without them. In fact, near the end of her life, as the Catholic Worker Movement progressed, Day often complained that though the new and younger workers were dedicated to the poor, they were not committed to the practices that enable such a life.

I've often excused my lack of disciplined spiritual practices by thinking, *I am an activist, a builder sort of guy.* Of course there were always plenty of people to celebrate this pattern in my life. And plenty of approaches to ministry tell us to "be who you are; be who God created you to be." Until I began to interact with the leaders of the spiritual formation movement, no one suggested that what Christian leaders bring to the table might be malformed and in need of transformation in order to live and lead as God intends. Dorothy Day did not suffer my ignorance on this topic. She is a classic example of a Christian who beautifully blended activism with spiritual practices.

DISPENSING BLESSING AND GRACE

For many readers Day's story may be overwhelming. The great majority of us will never have the scale of ministry and notoriety of Dorothy Day. God probably does not envision us living precisely as Day lived, but he does envision us blessing others as we have been blessed, on our own scale. Day demonstrates the connection between being blessed through the life and practices of the church—especially benediction—and the practice of blessing others. She is an inspiration and a model of this reality: the inaugurated kingdom of God is among us, and we get to participate in this good news by sharing it with others.

Those of us that find such a life a little scary need to know that "to follow Jesus . . . does not mean to solve every human problem—Christ himself did not attempt that—but it is rather to respond as he did, against all reason to dispense grace and love to those who deserve it least."

Trying to find a practical way forward, Philip Yancey looks to the oft-cited advice of Henry Nouwen, who says, "the goal of education and formation for the ministry is continually to recognize the Lord's voice, his face, and his touch in every person we meet." Day and Nouwen see things in similar ways: Jesus is somehow present in those who need the blessing we have received through benediction. Though this may not be easy, it is straightforward: we learn to pay attention, to take an interest in others, to be aware and present to the people and events of our life.

Once we get into this habit, we will be joyously surprised at the gifts and abilities that begin to flow through us as ambassadors of God's kingdom and love. Many of us do not regularly feel the power and authority of God because we do not regularly put ourselves out for others. As Eugene Peterson notes, "What we often consider to be the concerns of the spiritual life—ideas, truths, prayers, promises, beliefs—are never in the Christian gospel permitted to have a life of their own apart from particular persons and actual places." This is where teachers, ministers, police officers and public service people have the advantage: they are always around people in need. But all of us can do the same by volunteering or starting a hobby that puts us around people.

None of what we have been considering in this book works apart from the particular people and places that enter our lives. The reason we need to think about repracticing our faith is that millions of us have allowed church and our Christian lives to be compartmentalized from our daily routines. Our faith is reserved for Sunday morning. Our piety makes no difference in our everyday lives. We are blessed in the benediction and fearfully cling to it rather than pour it out.

Because the genuine spiritual life can be difficult, we excuse ourselves for these inconsistencies. But the watching world does not let us off the hook so easily. Most people expect to see a difference. If there is a God and if Christians truly commune with him and receive his blessing, that should make a difference in our lives in ways that our neighbors recognize and receive as good.

THE AARONIC BLESSING

The Aaronic Blessing, found in Numbers 6, has been spoken over God's people for thousands of years, and I believe it would help us to pick it up as spiritual practice. A fundamental truth about God becomes clear when we realize that God gave this blessing to Aaron: "Blessing is God's idea, his purpose. It is not something his people must beg for, but it is the outreaching of his grace." It rarely dawns on me, in any real and practical way, that grace and blessing are God's idea—even before creation. Creation itself is a self-giving act of God's favor, blessing and grace.

Let's look at what God intends for us through the Aaronic Blessing:

- The LORD bless you

    That is, may he give you favor and cause you to prosper richly in every good spiritual gift there is in Christ Jesus.

- and keep you

    May you know the goodness of God in action; may he guard you, watch over you and protect you. Implicit in this is that God has chosen you and he will go on with you.

- the LORD make his face shine upon you

    That is, may you sense the favor of your Creator God, that he is pleased with you. This harkens back to Moses on Sinai who experienced the dramatic presence and blessing of God.

- and be gracious to you

    May you be aware of God's forgiveness, compassion and mercy. May cowering fear of God be replaced with love for God as you experience his mercy.

- the LORD turn his face toward you

    That is, may he smile upon you. May you see in Jesus' face how much pleasure God takes in you and how very much God loves you and accepts you right where you are.

- and give you peace

    May you have *shalom*—the fullness of well-being. May you experience the sum of all the good God intends for his people; may you be at rest and centered in Christ Jesus, who is our Lord.

To Aaron, God says, "This is how you are to bless the Israelites. . . . And I will bless them." A benediction, given and received in faith, even in the most modest church, starts a river flowing with living water: from God, to his representative, to the people of God and finally to the least, the last and the left out. Benediction finds its deepest fulfillment when blessing is practiced for the sake of others. It was not meant to "remain merely a pious wish, . . . but to be manifested in the people with all the power of a blessing of God."

The Aaronic Blessing, these words given by God, is an outline for practicing compassion for others. Conveying this blessing in word or even the smallest deed is a potent repractice of an ancient Judeo-Christian observance. The authoritative and conceptual basis for repracticing benediction into blessing others is found in the way the original blessing was given. The divine blessing flows through the priest Aaron to the people of God. Today, we know that all Christians are priests, representatives and ambassadors of God. Therefore, we repractice benediction by letting blessing—divine favor and power—flow through us to others.

Conclusion

Putting the Spiritual Practices of the Church to Use

"The speed of gaining information is very fast,
but the speed of godliness is very slow."

JAMES HOUSTON

We've come to the time where this book is about to be put down and the spiritual practices of church picked up. As we do so, here is a tip: don't try to work with all the spiritual practices of church at once. Pick the one you feel most drawn to and begin there. It may take you months to move on. Speed is not the issue; deep and lasting change is. In an article I saw a couple years ago, a noted leader in the spiritual formation movement said:

> Well, I think the vocabulary [about speed] is wrong, be-
> cause it's all part of living in a technological society. And
> so processes, procedures, programs are all, in a sense,

technical devices or technical mindsets for fixing things. So we want to fix things quickly. But the very nature of integrity is that we have a speed that is appropriate to what we are doing. The speed of gaining information is very fast, but the speed of godliness is very slow. . . . So we lose integrity when we use the wrong mindset or the wrong speed at which we're operating. My problem is that I can think faster than I can speak, I speak faster than I can act, I've got more acts than I've got character for.

Though I want to quickly develop as Jesus' apprentice, I know that it's a lengthy process. I'm quite sure most Christians would agree that speed is not the most valued aspect of spiritual formation. Rather than pursuing speed, we need to foster a genuine desire to keep moving forward in repracticing a particular discipline of the church.

A counselor or friend who can function as a spiritual director might help us choose the practice that will be the most significant in our transformation. Once we have begun repracticing an element at church, we shouldn't move on until we know God is reshaping us into a different person. We can move on to another practice when our initial repracticing becomes natural and unself-conscious.

OUR EVERYDAY LIVES AS THE SOIL FOR REPRACTICING CHRISTIANITY

A refreshingly honest article in the *Wall Street Journal* undoubtedly speaks for millions of us:

I am by most measures a pretty deeply committed Christian. I am quite active in my church; I teach at a Christian college;

I have written extensively in support of Christian ideas and belief. Yet when I ask myself how much of what I do and think is driven by my religious beliefs, the honest answer is "not so much." The books I read, the food I eat, the music I listen to, my hobbies and interests, the thoughts that occupy my mind throughout the greater part of every day—these are, if truth be told, far less indebted to my Christianity than to my status as a middle-aged, middle-class American man.

I can relate to this person's candor. And thousands of conversations with fellow followers of Jesus tell me that author and I are not alone. Many of us are having a hard time practicing our Christianity in daily life. While modern life may make the possibility of a transforming encounter with God seem far off, it really isn't. For Scripture says, "in him we live and move and have our being" and God "is not far from each one of us" (Acts 17:27-28 NIV).

Nearly all people today identify themselves as "spiritual," and many of those same people would add "but not religious." In my experience what most people mean by this modifier is "I am not committed to any certain doctrine and not linked to any particular set of beliefs or practices."

This leads to the fact that rarely do "spiritual but not religious" people have a good grasp of the teachings of Jesus and how they might apply to contemporary issues. Most of these people know very little about the Bible, doctrine, church history and theology. And every survey suggests that this pattern is becoming more pronounced every year.

The spiritual inability and disablement this leads to is rooted in a lack of understanding. *But*, you might protest, *in this book we have been talking about practices, not intellectual work.* I have three responses.

First, it is true that thinking alone does not bring understanding and growth. Anyone who has ever learned a sport, a hobby or a new language knows that thinking only gets a person so far. At some point we need to *practice* what we are thinking.

Second, though we have been discussing practices, this does not mean that thinking well theologically (i.e., understanding and believing as accurately as we can) is a bad thing or a wrong pursuit. Millions of Christians will testify that studying the Bible, church history, theology and biblical languages benefits them greatly! The *problem* with such learning is that without accompanying spiritual practices, lives remain stunted. Having intellectual learning without practices is like having a sports car without wheels. This is what has given the academy a bad rap.

Third, all practices have a rational or thinking component. For instance, the transformation of tithing to living with simplicity requires not just a change of heart but some planning as well. Repracticing quiet times may require studying the person and work of the Holy Spirit. The same is true of all the practices; each has a cognitive element.

Understanding—through mental and bodily work—has the power to facilitate growth in any endeavor. Think about it: the things we understand the least—perhaps math or a foreign language or speaking in public—are the things we least like to do and are least committed to.

REPRACTICING CHURCH HAPPENS
FROM THE INSIDE OUT

There is a counterintuitive aspect of engaging with the spiritual practices of church. Though spiritual formation is chiefly an inward reality, we often work on our heart, mind and soul through bodily or external practices. This is true of all the spiritual practices of church. But we need to keep in mind that it is the inward part of our life from which outward actions flow.

At least three of Jesus' parables inform us that spiritual formation happens inside out. For instance, he said some of the religious leaders of his day were like whitewashed tombs (Matthew 23:27). There is nothing wrong with caring for the tombs of loved ones. (I learned this lesson from watching my mother lovingly care for my brother's burial site.) Jesus' point is that such commonly practiced behavior, perfectly fine in its own right, leaves the inside of the tomb, the crucial bit, untouched—still filled with death. He was telling the religious leaders that their approach to spiritual transformation was inherently flawed. Spiritual formation does not happen from the outside in but the inside out. The spiritual practices of church are bodily, or "external." But the growth and transformation they produce begin on the inside—the heart, as Jesus says—and then that change is expressed in new behaviors.

When Jesus said that our words come from the overflow or abundance of our heart (Matthew 12:34), he was making the same point—the inner guides the outer; the outer should be an accurate reflection of the inner life. When he said a bad tree cannot produce good fruit (Matthew 7:17-18), same point again—the inner DNA of the tree produces the fruit on the tree. Last, Jesus used a lesson from dishwashing. He said it was wrongheaded to wash the outside of a cup while leaving the inside dirty (Matthew 23:25-26). Picture your favorite coffee mug or stainless-steel travel tumbler stained on the inside from a long day of work. To clean it, you fill it about a third full with hot water, pump a few squirts of dish soap in it and scrub like mad until the stains are gone. In the process lots of watery soap bubbles will flow to the outside of the cup. As you rinse and dry the cup, the outside will be cleaned as a byproduct of the inner effort.

When we embark on the journey toward repracticing our faith, we will experience more deeply the tug of war *inside* us. We'll want to revisit Jesus' words and work in conjunction with them. Through their application, our dreams of engaging with the spiritual practices of church in order to be the cooperative friends of Jesus can come true.

THE SPIRITUAL PRACTICES OF CHURCH: A TOOL FOR EVANGELISM

Repracticing Christianity is crucial for evangelism today. In my experience, today's seekers often *observe* their way into faith. This is a big shift that has become pronounced in the last five to ten years. As a professor of evangelism, I have wondered for years why this is so. Lesslie Newbigin's work has helped me a great deal. He is an expert guide for post-Christian realities. This being the first time the church has had to mount a mission to a culture that was previously Christian, we need expert guides like Newbigin.

Previously Christian! Think about that. Picture someone saying "I used to own an XYZ car, but I'd never buy one again!" Or "I tried that product on television. They even doubled the amount I received, but it didn't work." Can you imagine how hard it would be to sell those people the same products again! While I don't like linking marketing to the gospel, in this instance it is instructive. America is full of people who tried "the Christian thing" and found it wanting, or people who need to see something *real*, something that really *works* and don't think they will find it in the church.

It used to be that seekers mainly *listened* their way into faith. This was a time marked by a consensus regarding the basic goodness and reliability of Christianity. Moreover, there was a common language inside and outside the church through which we could discuss religious and spiritual matters. When this situation existed—when seekers were mostly listening to a language they at least vaguely understood—the evangelistic role of Christians was to talk. And boy did we get good at talking! So much so that the culture is now asking us to please be quiet! But this request does not indicate a lack of interest in spiritual things. Today, people first desire community and belonging. Dialogue and conversation, mutual and respectful discussion about faith come later.

As they *see* something in the Christians they have contact with, seekers become open to faith and following Jesus. The way we treat them in conversations about faith, the Bible, world religions, the exclusivity of Jesus and the like is critical. So are our practices. Chuck Smith, my first mentor in the Bible, often said, "You are always being a witness; the only question is are you being a good one or a poor, unhelpful, drive-people-away one?"

This is why repracticing our faith in winsome ways is so important. Imagine seekers being able to notice us living the *eucharistic life* for the sake of others; observe us moving from arguing about the Bible to embodying its story, and experiencing our quiet times as a launching pad for practicing the presence of God in our whole day.

PRACTICES FOR SEEKERS AND THE DECHURCHED

In the preface I candidly said that my journey into repracticed Christianity began with a crisis of faith. I never doubted the reality of God or my life-receiving connection to God, but just about everything else was shaken. Eighteen years ago I might have been one of the "unchurched Harrys" we hear a lot about today, but I couldn't leave the church—I was the pastor! So I served God and my congregation well and began to pursue my own spiritual transformation by discovering and repracticing the spiritual practices of church.

My religious crisis came many years into my walk with Christ. Maybe you've been so stuck in your thinking that you've never really begun to believe. If, however, you want to believe, if you are a seeker, let me suggest a road other than the one you have been taking: try finding faith through the spiritual practices of the church. Coming to right belief will be a byproduct. As a way to find faith, it is definitely a road less traveled, but that is a comment on us, not the road.

The vast majority of us, because of the way the gospel has been preached in our generation, have thought that faith equals doctrinal agreement. But it doesn't work that way in the Bible. Abraham followed God long before he had a good theological grasp of what was going on. The disciples, while actively engaged in following Jesus, learned doctrinal truth and a new way to read and understand the Jewish Scriptures *as they went along.*

As they went along. These are vitally important, vision-casting words for those who are trying to find faith—or trying to find it again. I have often observed a fly trying to get out a closed window by crashing into it every couple of seconds when just across the kitchen the door to the back yard is wide open. Some of us have been approaching faith that way—hitting our heads over and over again on the window of *trying to believe.* Why not fly over to the open door and do what the characters in the Bible did—practice your way into faith.

WHAT TO DO ABOUT CHURCH?

Some of us may have gained a clear vision for a different kind of life in Christ but are still unclear or unconvinced about the church. Should we go back to church? Why? How? These are real and important questions, so let's take a moment with each one:

Should we go to church? Yes, but church reconceived as the pregame meeting, not the game itself.

Why? Church is the place to engage in important spiritual practices that have nourished followers of Jesus for thousands of years.

How? By putting *church* in its place. The kingdom of God—God's action on earth—is the uppermost point of loyalty for Christians. The action of God creates the church, the called and sent people of God. After the ascension of Christ, the sending of the Spirit and the creation of the church, the church became the primary means through which God's action is expressed. Through the spiritual practices of church we are being trained as ambassadors of God's kingdom. This is the vision for my life as both a pastor and a follower of Jesus.

I have presented a way to engage in the spiritual practices of church—one marked by peace, joy and ease rather than angst, guilt and neurotic effort. I hope you will give the church another chance. Try repracticing the historic routines of the church as a springboard into new life. These historic practices are not without power. On the contrary, they have survived the centuries precisely because of their life-giving qualities. They have transformed millions of seekers, the dechurched and the barely churched into followers of Jesus for the sake of others.

Group Exercises

INTRODUCTION

- Have you experienced a time when your views and feelings about church were primarily negative? Tell your story.

- If you are reading this book, you clearly are willing to give church another chance. Why? What has been happening in your mind or heart to make you open to learning about the spiritual practices of church?

- Describe what you imagine it might look like to not just "use Jesus' words in Bible studies" (*The Message*).

- Can you imagine what it means to "repractice" the elements of church as a springboard to life? Describe how that might work.

CHAPTER 1: GOING TO CHURCH

- Discuss the author's notion that church is not "the game," but the meeting that prepares us for a life.

- Interact with the author's notions about how beliefs and practices are meant to work together.

- Brainstorm some ways that you can be a "sent person of God" in the already existing activities of your life.

- Perhaps you have heard for years that there is nothing to *do* in the Christian life—that Jesus did it all. While that is true with reference to the forgiveness of sins, can you imagine a way to *live* without the spirit of doing that underlies a misguided need to earn the love of God?

- Discuss this scenario: maybe like some of the early followers of Jesus, you are unsure about "risking it all." Yet Jesus still sent his first friends. He is sending you now. Consider ways you can respond even in your semi-faith state.

- Describe what you think it might mean to be an ambassador of the kingdom of God in doable ways (like Debbie) within the life you now experience day in and day out.

CHAPTER 2: QUIET PRELUDE

- Do you ever want silence and solitude? Why do you suppose that hunger arises? What benefits do you expect would come from silence? Be as concrete and clear as possible about these questions as you share with your group or partner.

- Connecting the spiritual practices of church to our actual existing life is the major theme of this book. Can you imagine connecting the quiet of preludes to your present life? How might that work?

- Can you relate to being "thrilled to death"? Do you find yourself needing more and more of your favorite "stuff" to be satisfied? Envision out loud how pursuing a life that includes quiet times might deliver you from the oppression of needing to be constantly "thrilled."

- Can you begin to construct in your mind a way to "work from the basis of rest" instead of always just getting by exhausted all the time?

- Imagine out loud what it might be like to walk in Jesus' "unforced rhythms of grace," in which you live "freely and lightly." Does this seem doable to you? What are the largest obstacles you see for such a life?

- What might it look like to live with Sabbath and work as a unified whole?

CHAPTER 3: SINGING THE DOXOLOGY

- While none of us are likely to be as bright as floodlights shining hundreds of feet in the air, can you imagine the possibility of reflecting something of the glory of God as that beautiful chorus goes around in your head? Discuss how this might occur.

- What if you could do this without adding any busyness to your existing life? What if what you already did every day could count if you just brought into it the reality of doxology? This can—and has to—happen. Describe how it could become real in your life.

- Ponder and discuss this idea: your present life—with all its ups and downs and challenges and opportunities—is designed by God to be a light, something that cannot be hid even if you tried! Discuss how this could happen without adding a bunch of religious activity—just a simple chorus—to your already over-busy life.

- Which line from the Doxology is your favorite? Why? What vision does it impart for life? What hope does it give you?

How does it orient your thinking and behavior toward God?

CHAPTER 4: SCRIPTURE READING

- In your estimation have you spent more time trying to master the Bible than seeking to be mastered by it? Where did you get the idea to focus on the former to the semi-exclusion of the latter? How might you switch the emphasis?

- Bring the events of today to mind—or the events planned for tomorrow: how can you immerse them in the story of the Bible? Do you see a difference-making shift here? Rather than trying to fit a verse of the Bible to our lives, we take our whole lives and baptize them—immerse them—in God's story. Discuss how this could actually happen.

- Do you have any negative feelings toward the Bible? If so, find a safe place to bring your thoughts before others. God will not be shocked—he already knows what you are thinking! Ask your group to be patient with you as you unpack some baggage you have with reference to the Scriptures.

- Do you agree with Dallas Willard that the crucial attitude for reading the Bible is "an attitude of submission"? Like the author, do you sometimes struggle with the notion of obedience? Do you tend to read the Bible for mere information? Do you read it with a sense of mysticism—that "something good should happen if I read the Bible"? What would it take for you to read the Bible with a heart toward submission—toward fitting your life into the story you read in the Bible?

- Discuss how the following statement could be true: reading the Bible can lead to "skill for living."

- Jesus talked about obedience being "food to his soul." Think aloud together about how such satisfaction could be a reality for you.

- Discuss how a "poor man's Bible" could generate a rich spiritual life. Reflect on how the story of God, as pictured in stained glass, may be the source of the spiritual life you seek.

CHAPTER 5: HEARING SERMONS

- "Blah, blah, blah" you hear in your ears for 30 to 45 minutes. Are you tired of or bored with sermons? Why? Soberly think about it—without malice: what is going wrong so often today between preacher and hearer?

- What do you think of the author's idea that the break between preacher and hearer has to do with loss of story and the intention to act on what we hear?

- Everyone is learning to do life from someone: who is teaching you your economic, sexual, relational ethics? Have you ever thought about this? As you do think about it, what do you notice or learn?

- Do you agree with the author that, when all else fails and you do not know for sure what to do, Jesus' Golden Rule is a good place to begin for obedience?

- Have you ever considered the idea that the narrow way is the easy way—that the disobedient life is actually the hard life? Discuss the implications of the idea.

- What might change if the next time you heard a sermon you asked: "how can I get in on the story from which this sermon has been lifted?"

CHAPTER 6: FOLLOWING LITURGY

- Discuss a few ideas for taking weekly worship (liturgy) "public," for using it as a launching pad for your actual life.

- Have you thought of your vocation as your job? What changes if you reconsider your job as merely that for which you get a paycheck? What changes if you understand your vocation as your calling from God to be his special and sent people at your job?

- What would happen if we moved prayer books from the back of pews to our coffee tables or nightstands or wherever you read? Discuss what it could look like to use the prayer book or daily offices the way they were designed—to, under the guidance and authority of the Word and the Spirit, direct the spiritual life.

- Discuss what you might do to repractice liturgy so that it shapes and gives rhythm to your life.

- What did you think of the author's connection between liturgy and evangelism? Do you agree that most seekers today are observing their way into faith more than questioning their way in?

CHAPTER 7: GIVING AN OFFERING

- What do you think about the author's vision for a simple life? How do you feel about it on an emotional level? Describe how you can see duplicity and complexity as anxiety producing.

- Do you believe tithing/giving is a quid pro quo with God? Why or why not? If giving is not an "economic exchange" with God, how should we understand the biblical passages that suggest that God blesses those who give? What do you suppose is the "sweet spot" between a deal with God and God's desire to bless generous giving?

- Discuss the list of challenges the author suggests on page 131: what do you think about them?

- The author asserts that proper thinking about Christian giving should emerge from the overall story of the Bible, not just a couple proof-texts. Do you agree? If so, in what direction does that story point our giving?

CHAPTER 8: TAKING COMMUNION

- Discuss among yourselves how routine, faith-filled participation in Communion might create, shape, enliven and empower a life of thankfulness that in turn spills over to others.

- If, as the quote from N. T. Wright on page 135 says, "in the Eucharist . . . through the death and resurrection of Jesus Christ, [the] future dimension is brought sharply into play," what could that mean? How might it affect our thinking, attitudes and behaviors?

- If you were raised in a liturgical church, you may have connected easily with the author's thoughts about Communion being boring rather than inspiring and enabling a life "for the sake of others." Discuss why some people are empowered by Communion while others find it rote and meaningless.

- Discuss the author's connection of Communion to the towel of Jesus—to serving others as an overflow of Eucharistic thankfulness.

- Discuss various ways in which Eucharist can, in your daily life, move from a noun to a verb.

CHAPTER 9: RECEIVING THE BENEDICTION

- Discuss ways in which a fresh interaction with the benediction can lead us from church as "I understand or believe" to church as "I will go."

- Discuss the author's suggestion that the sixteenth-century reformers were mostly concerned with producing a different sort of Christian *life*—that the doctrinal corrections they brought to bear were not mere abstractions but concrete foundations meant to shape a way of living.

- The "blessed" life the author suggests leads to an ongoing cycle: we are blessed in benediction, we bless others. What would be the thoughts, attitudes and actions associated with that cycle?

- Can you imagine seeing Jesus in the eyes of the needy? How might such a reality simultaneously disciple you and bless others?

- Dorothy Day insisted throughout her life that the spiritual practices of church empowered her ministry among the poor, sick and marginalized. Discuss how this might work for you.

- Look again at the various phrases in the Aaronic Blessing on page 157. Discuss how each could become reality for your life.

CONCLUSION

- The author suggests that we should not try to repractice all the elements of church at once—that we should chose the one to which we think the Holy Spirit is pointing us. Which practice is that for you, and why?

- In order to best go on the journey, the author suggests that we make use of a spiritual director, friend, companion or guide. Do you have one? Why or why not? If not, discuss ways in which you might find such a person.

- The author wants our repracticing of church to overflow into our daily lives as the biblical passage from Romans 12 suggests. Enumerate one or two ways in which you can do this right away.

- The author says that repracticing church toward a different kind of life happens from the inside out. Discuss the sayings of Jesus on page 163, and imagine aloud how they could work in practice for you.

- Because many seekers are observing their way into the faith, the author envisions repracticed Christianity as a major tool for evangelism in the years ahead. Do you agree? Why or why not?

- You've finished the book: will you reengage the spiritual practices of church? If yes, what do you hope to experience? If no, what would it take for you to engage with the spiritual practices of church?

Notes

Preface

p. 19   "vendors of religious goods and services": I am indebted to my friend who wrote *Missional Church* for the shocking and powerful phrase "vendors of religious goods and services." Darrell Guder, ed., *Missional Church* (Grand Rapids: Eerdmans, 1998), pp. 201-2.

p. 20   "God has spoken; everything else is commentary—right?": This saying appears several times in Rob Bell's *Velvet Elvis* (Grand Rapids: Zondervan, 2005).

Introduction

p. 33   "not a practice-oriented religion but a Sunday religion": Peter Senge, "Exploring Off the Map," hosted by Leadership Network, May 23-26, 2000. Several weeks after writing this chapter, while still doing some research for this book, I picked up Brian McLaren's book *Finding Our Way Again: The Return of the Ancient Practices.* I was surprised to see that Brian tells this same story in his book, but from the point of view of the host conducting the interview with Dr. Senge. It was fascinating and fun for me to hear Brain tell the same story through slightly different eyes. You may want to check it out too.

p. 35   not the place for a long discussion on truth: Crystal L. Downing has written an important book on the subject of truth titled *How Postmodernism Serves (My) Faith* (Downers Grove, Ill.: InterVarsity Press, 2006).

p. 36   "life, life and more life": As Eugene Peterson translates the
         Greek NT phrase for "eternal life." See, for instance, Luke
         19:26; John 10:6; Romans 5:20; 6:22; Philippians 3:20; Titus
         3:3. See also Eugene H. Peterson, *Christ Plays in Ten Thousand
         Places: A Conversation in Spiritual Theology* (Grand Rapids:
         Eerdmans, 2005), p. 1.

p. 37   "When the church is seen to move straight from worship":
         N. T. Wright, *Surprised by Hope* (New York: HarperOne,
         2008), p. 267.

Chapter 1: Going to Church

p. 41   right stuff, accurate beliefs and correct ingredients: Brian
         McLaren conveys a great analogy regarding how we can have
         all the right ingredients for a cake, but use the wrong prac-
         tices, the wrong way of making the cake and thus have an
         inedible cake (*Finding Our Way Again* [Nashville: Thomas
         Nelson, 2008], pp. 55-56).

p. 43   "a life-long process of separating church from God": Philip
         Yancey, *Soul Survivor* (New York: Doubleday, 2001), p. 45.

p. 44   Millions of Americans are also leaving cool churches: See for
         instance Christine Wicker, *The Fall of the Evangelical Nation*
         (New York: HarperOne, 2008); George Barna, *Revolutionaries*
         (Wheaton, Ill.: Tyndale, 2005); Julia Duin, *Quitting Church*
         (Grand Rapids: Baker, 2008); and David T. Olson, *The Ameri-
         can Church in Crisis* (Grand Rapids: Zondervan, 2008).

p. 44   "Union in action with the Triune God is Christian spiritual-
         ity": Dallas Willard, *The Great Omission* (New York: Harper-
         SanFrancisco, 2006), p. 52.

p. 44   our problems come from picking and choosing: See Scot
         McKnight, *The Blue Parakeet* (Grand Rapids: Zondervan,
         2008).

p. 45   "No matter how right we are in what we believe": Eugene Pe-
         terson, *Christ Plays in Ten Thousand Places* (London: Hodder
         & Stoughton, 2005), p. 261.

p. 45   "prepositional-participation . . . of *with, in* and *for*": Ibid., p.
         335.

p. 48   "buildings are not the problem": Mark Foreman, *Wholly Jesus*
         (Boise: Ampelon, 2008).

p. 48   God is not interested in our *buildings* and *styles*. See for instance Frank Viola, *Pagan Christianity* (Wheaton, Ill.: Tyndale, 2008); Michael Frost and Alan Hirsch, *The Shaping of Things to Come* (Peabody, Mass.: Hendrickson, 2003); and Alan Hirsch, *The Forgotten Ways* (Grand Rapids: Brazos, 2006). These books also have extensive bibliographies allowing one to follow the most relevant streams of thought. I want to say here that I am not minimizing their work. I respect them and have learned from them and expect to continue to learn from them. But I see a synthesis coming. First there was the 1970s-1990s church growth movement (including the seeker movement). Then in the last decade or so there has been a counterpoint to this movement. Now I see something new coming into view: a way of being the people of God that makes mission such a powerful social-psychological force that meetings and buildings will be set in their proper places as means, not ends.

p. 49   "viewed themselves as a transformational kingdom force": Foreman, *Wholly Jesus*, p. 189.

p. 49   "We have everything reversed": Ibid.

p. 50   "house churches can be just as guilty": Ibid., pp. 189, 190.

p. 50   Todd's new church plant: Holy Trinity Anglican Church, Costa Mesa, California. See <www.myholytrinitychurch.com>.

p. 50   "Church size, polity, style and building must follow function": Foreman, *Wholly Jesus*, p. 202.

p. 52   He introduced me to Mother Teresa: John Wimber, *Kingdom Ministry* (Ann Arbor, Mich.: Servant, 1987), pp. 29-31.

p. 52   "We learn how to be servants of the master": Ibid., pp. 31-32.

p. 52   Gospel and Our Culture Network: see <www.gocn.org>.

Chapter 2: Quiet Prelude

p. 59   "Spirituality is not immaterial as opposed to material": Eugene Peterson, *Christ Plays in Ten Thousand Places* (London: Hodder & Stoughton, 2005), p. 30.

p. 60   "The end of all Christian belief and obedience": Ibid., p. 1 (emphasis added).

p. 60   "If we are going to *live* as intended": Ibid., p. 84 (emphasis added).

p. 61   "the hijacking of the brain's pleasure system": Archibald Hart, *Thrilled to Death: How the Endless Pursuit of Pleasure Is Leaving Us Numb* (Nashville: Thomas Nelson, 2007), p. xii.

p. 62   private mediation and corporate worship: I am not endorsing non-Christian or anti-Christian uses of meditation. I mean it in its plainest sense: the intellectual activities associated with pondering or thinking deeply about something. There is actually a long evangelical tradition of mediating on Scripture (see ibid., p. 220). On corporate worship see ibid., p. xiii.

p. 62   focusing on the presence of God: Ibid., p. 218.

p. 62   worship full of intensity and stimulation driven: Ibid., p. 219.

p. 62   "stimulation-driven spirituality is not conducive to lowered stress": Ibid., p. 220.

p. 63   geared to our times and anchored to the Rock: "Anchored to the Rock . . . Geared to the Times" is the very helpful motto of Youth For Christ.

pp. 65-66   "Work does not take us away from God": Peterson, *Christ Plays in Ten Thousand Places*, p. 115.

p. 66   "our Adversary majors in three things": Richard J. Foster, *Celebration of Discipline* (New York: Harper & Row, 1978), p. 13.

p. 66   the contemplative life is not solitary: See renovare.org for an introduction to what Foster has called "a balanced vision" of the six practices of Jesus.

p. 66   "no spirituality, no God-attentive, God-responsive life": Peterson, *Christ Plays in Ten Thousand Places*, pp. 117-18.

p. 66   Compassionate life, virtuous life, evangelical life, etc.: See <www.renovare.org> for more on these five streams.

Chapter 3: Singing the Doxology

pp. 71-72   Three Is Enough Groups: See chapter ten of my *Christianity Beyond Belief* (Downers Grove, Ill.: InterVarsity Press, 2009). See also <www.3isenough.org>.

p. 75   Dallas Willard on radiating the nature of God: Dallas Willard, *The Great Omission* (New York: HarperSanFrancisco, 2006), p. 124.

p. 76   "Emphasis on the wickedness and neediness": Ibid., p. 206.

p. 77   marvelous by design and purpose, but presently damaged: Ibid., pp. 206-7.

p. 79   Thomas Ken wrote the doxology in 1674: Clyde Curry Smith, "Doxology," in *The New International Dictionary of the Church*, ed. J. D. Douglas (Grand Rapids: Zondervan, 1978), p. 312.

p. 79   Ken wrote the doxology under controversial conditions: See "Doxology," *Dr. Chadwick's Church Ministry Site* <www.joy fulministry.com/doxolf.htm>.

p. 80   Yes. Yes. Yes. This is the way Eugene Peterson sometimes translates *amen* in *The Message*. See Matthew 6:7.

p. 81   bringing glory to God is a form of doxology: Albert Mauder, "Doxology," in *The Encyclopedia of Christianity* (Grand Rapids: Eerdmans, 1997), p. 885.

Chapter 4: Scripture Reading

p. 83   *Invisible Children:* See <www.invisiblechildren.com>.

p. 84   Todd's son Jonathan: See Jonathan's remarks on pages 122-23.

p. 85   "Anglicans hearing more of the Word of God": William Wolf, John Booty and Owen Thomas, *The Spirit of Anglicanism* (Harrisburg, Penn.: Morehouse, 1979), p. 175

p. 87   "We will be spiritually safe": Dallas Willard, *Hearing God* (Downers Grove, Ill.: InterVarsity Press, 1999), p. 161.

p. 87   "new life in the Spirit, in obedience to the lordship of Jesus Christ": N. T. Wright, *Surprised by Hope* (New York: HarperOne, 2008), p. 221.

p. 89   brief overview of *Missional Church:* See the key points in *Missional Church*, ed. Darrell Guder (Grand Rapids: Eerdmans, 1998), chap. 4.

pp. 90-91   baseball and music illustrations: I first encountered the notion of reading and acting on the Bible in this way from N. T. Wright, who I believe uses the illustration of a Shakespearean play or a missing bit of a symphony. Unfortunately I cannot remember where I read it.

p. 91   "Biblical spirituality/religion has a low tolerance for 'great ideas'": Eugene Peterson, *Christ Plays in Ten Thousand Places* (London: Hodder & Stoughton, 2005), p. 115.

p. 92   "the primary location for spiritual formation is the workplace": Ibid., p. 127.

p. 92   "Story is the most natural way": Ibid., p. 13.

p. 92   "The biblical way is not to present us a moral code": Ibid., p. 140 (emphasis added).

p. 95   "living the Bible as story": Scot McKnight, *The Blue Parakeet* (Grand Rapids: Zondervan, 2008), p. 12.

p. 95   "If you are doing good works, you are reading the Bible aright": Ibid., p. 113.

p. 96   the Bible as a family scrapbook or photo album: See Rob Bell, *Velvet Elvis* (Grand Rapids: Zondervan, 2005), pp. 58-63.

Chapter 5: Hearing Sermons

p. 100   "My deepest doubts about the faith": Philip Yancey, *Soul Survivor* (New York: Doubleday, 2001), p. 119.

p. 102   encourage people to wear the yoke of the Torah: N. T. Wright, *Matthew for Everyone* (London: SPCK, 2002), p. 137.

p. 103   Jesus carries most of the load: Craig S. Keener, *Matthew*, IVP New Testament Commentary (Downers Grove, Ill.: InterVarsity Press, 1997), pp. 222-23.

p. 103   We all make a radical choice: Modified from Dallas Willard, *The Great Omission* (New York: HarperSanFrancisco, 2006), p. 226.

p. 105   normal in God's new society: *God's New Society* is the name of John Stott's commentary on Ephesians (Downers Grove, Ill.: InterVarsity Press, 1979).

pp. 105-6   "no dirty minds among us expressing themselves in dirty words": Ibid., p. 192.

pp. 107-8   Yancey's conversation with *Pravda* leaders: Philip Yancey, *The Jesus I Never Knew* (Grand Rapids: Zondervan, 1998), p. 75.

p. 108   "the story so far" and "how it is supposed to end": N. T. Wright, *Surprised by Hope* (New York: HarperOne, 2008), p. 281.

p. 109   the Trinity's dialogue: William P. Young, *The Shack* (Newbury Park, Calif.: Windblown Media, 2007), pp. 209-10.

p. 110   "Who am I and what people think I am": Eugene Peterson, *Christ Plays in Ten Thousand Places* (London: Hodder & Stoughton, 2005), p. 15.

p. 110   "The work of the Spirit in creation is no longer confined": Ibid., pp. 22-23.

p. 111   spiritual *practices* make possible the way: Thanks to Brian

McLaren for the thought I am riffing on here. See his *Finding
Our Way Again* (Nashville: Thomas Nelson, 2008), p. 34.

Chapter 6: Following Liturgy

p. 114   "the prescribed service of Eucharist": "Liturgy," in *The Oxford
Dictionary of the Christian Church* (Oxford: Oxford University
Press, 1983), p. 830.

p. 115   a loving mother with newborn baby: P. D. Manson, "Wor-
ship," in *New Dictionary of Theology*, ed. Sinclair B. Ferguson,
J. I. Packer and David F. Wright (Downers Grove, Ill.: Inter-
Varsity Press, 1988), p. 730.

p. 117   whole-life understanding is our covenant with God: Robert
Banks and R. Paul Stevens, "Worship," in *The Complete Book
of Everyday Theology* (Downers Grove, Ill.: InterVarsity Press,
1997), p. 1141.

p. 117   new covenant deepens and empowers the earlier covenant:
Ibid.

p. 117   Worship as "an orientation to life": Ibid.

p. 120   belief and doctrine begin and end in worship and prayer:
D. E. Saliers, "Liturgical Theology," in *The Westminster Dic-
tionary of Christian Theology*, ed. Alan Richardson and John
Bowden (Philadelphia: Westminster Press, 1983), p. 336.

Chapter 7: Giving an Offering

p. 129   *simplicity* is freedom; *duplicity* is bondage: Richard Foster, *Celebration of Discipline* (San Francisco: Harper & Row, 1978), p. 69.

p. 129   "*Simplicity* brings freedom and joy": Ibid.

p. 130   "Compulsive extravagance is a modern mania": Richard Foster, *The Challenge of the Disciplined Life* (New York: Harper-
Collins, 1985), p. 5.

p. 130   "the sheer fact that a person is living without things": Foster,
Celebration of Discipline, pp. 76-77.

p. 131   money has character and power: Foster, *Challenge of the Disciplined Life*, pp. 24-25.

p. 131   use Mammon without serving Mammon: Ibid., p. 56.

p. 131   Fosteresque challenges: See chapter five of *Challenge of the
Disciplined Life*. Here I am quoting loosely and commenting
on what I have learned from Foster.

p. 132   Ancient Israel's robbing of God: John Walton, Victor Mat-
thews and Mark Chavalas, *The IVP Bible Background Com-
mentary: Old Testament* (Downers Grove, Ill.: InterVarsity
Press, 2000), p. 810; see also Walter C. Kaiser Jr., *Micah–
Malachi*, vol. 21, The Communicator's Commentary (Dallas:
Word, 1992), pp. 476ff.

p. 133   should tithing be on gross or net income?: I did a search on
Amazon.com that turned up fifty books on tithing, which
probably represents every perspective imaginable.

p. 134   reading the Bible as story: See Scot McKnight, *The Blue Parakeet* (Grand Rapids: Zondervan, 2008) for a clear and read-
able introduction to the Bible as story.

Chapter 8: Taking Communion

p. 136   the meaning of Eucharist: In this chapter, I use the term *Eucharist* because it is the common term of the Anglican tradition. In so doing, I mean no disrespect to other traditions—
from the Catholics on one side and "memorialists" on the
other. This is not the place for me to enter that debate. I have
no interest or need in this context to explore the various con-
troversies over what happens with the elements—the bread
and wine—or the mode of Christ's presence during Eucharist. Rather, I ask readers to work their tradition into a life of
thankfulness. However, if you are interested, a great overview is found in Gordon T. Smith, ed., *The Lord's Supper: Five
Views* (Downers Grove, Ill.: InterVarsity Press, 2008). For a
classic Anglican view, see John W. Howe, *Our Anglican Heritage* (Eugene, Ore.: Wipf & Stock, 2007). For a more evangelical Anglican view, I suggest finding teaching by John
Stott or J. I. Packer, though I am not aware of any specific
book sources.

p. 136   twofold thanks of the Eucharist: "Eucharist," in *The Oxford
Dictionary of the Christian Church* (Oxford: Oxford University
Press, 1983), p. 475.

p. 137   a real continuation in the life of Christ: Ronald S. Wallace,
"Communion, Holy," *The New International Dictionary of the
Christian Church,* ed. J. D. Douglas, E. Earle Cairns and James E.
Ruark (Grand Rapids: Zondervan, 1978), p. 244.

p. 137   Jesus' life and the Eucharist are eschatological events: escha-
          tology has to do with the progression, direction and purpose
          of redemptive history as it moves toward its ultimate climax,
          the consummation of the Kingdom of God (Stanley J. Grenz,
          David Guretzki and Cherith Fee Nordling, "Eschatology,"
          The Pocket Dictionary of Theological Terms [Downers Grove,
          Ill.: InterVarsity Press, 1999], p. 46).

p. 137   "this would be laughable if it wasn't happening": N. T. Wright,
          Surprised by Hope (New York: HarperOne, 2008), p. 227.

p. 138   sacrifice is integral to Eucharist: We will not engage in the
          arguments regarding the nature of sacrifice inherent in the
          covenant meal. I suggest that interested readers pick up a dic-
          tionary of theology and follow the argument there.

p. 140   taking of Communion unworthily: I am using the term *un-
          worthy* in the Pauline sense of 1 Corinthians 11.

p. 142   "within the sacramental world, past and present are one":
          Wright, *Surprised by Hope*, p. 274.

p. 142   "spirituality that is dominated by ideas about Jesus": Ibid., p.
          203.

p. 145   Holy Trinity Church, Costa Mesa: As I was writing this book
          in 2009, I was, with the help of wonderful associate pastors
          in each place, simultaneously planting churches in Boise,
          Idaho, and Costa Mesa. Both churches are named Holy Trin-
          ity Church and are aligned with The Anglican Mission in the
          Americas. I presently live in Boise and commute to Costa
          Mesa. The plan is for our family to move to Costa Mesa in the
          summer of 2010.

p. 145   God "did not want to rescue humans *from* creation": Wright,
          Surprised by Hope, p. 202.

Chapter 9: Receiving the Benediction

p. 148   "Christianity was no longer a power to be experienced": Rob-
          ert Webber, *Evangelicals on the Canterbury Trail* (Harrisburg,
          Penn.: Morehouse, 1985), pp. 24-25.

p. 149   "They were convinced that the new understanding": Stephen
          Neill, *Anglicanism* (New York: Oxford University Press, 1976),
          p. 50.

p. 150   "The layman also is called to be a saint": Ibid., p. 51.

p. 151   "awareness of the world's castoff people haunted her": Jim Forest, *Love Is the Measure* (New York: Paulist, 1986), p. 15.

p. 153   common church practices enabled Day's sacrificial life: Ibid., p. 80.

p. 154   younger workers were not committed to the practices: Ibid., pp. 130, 140.

p. 154   blending activism with spiritual practices: See Brian McLaren, *Finding Our Way Again* (Nashville: Thomas Nelson, 2008), p. 72, for a discussion of the interactive role of activism and contemplation.

p. 155   "to follow Jesus . . . does not mean to solve every human problem": Philip Yancey, *Soul Survivor* (New York: Doubleday, 2001), p. 142.

p. 155   "the goal of education and formation for the ministry": Henry Nouwen, quoted in ibid., p. 315.

p. 155   "What we often consider to be the concerns of the spiritual life": Eugene Peterson, *Christ Plays in Ten Thousand Places* (London: Hodder & Stoughton, 2005), p. 75.

p. 156   "Blessing is God's idea, his purpose": Walter C. Kaiser Jr., *Exodus,* vol. 2, Expositor's Bible Commentary, ed. Frank E. Gaebelein (Grand Rapids: Zondervan, 1990), p. 754.

p. 157   May you know the goodness of God in action: C. F. Keil and F. Delitzsch, *The Pentateuch,* Biblical Commentary on the Old Testament (Grand Rapids: Eerdmans, 1980), p. 41.

p. 157   may you sense the favor of your Creator God: Ibid., p. 755.

p. 157   may he smile upon you: Ibid.

p. 157   the sum of all the good God intends for his people: Ibid., p. 41.

p. 158   "It was not meant to "remain merely a pious wish": Ibid., p. 42.

Conclusion

p. 159   "I think the vocabulary [about speed] is wrong": James Houston, *Denver Seminary Magazine,* summer 2006, p. 6.

pp. 160-61 "I am by most measures a pretty deeply committed Christian": Alan Jacobs, "Too Much Faith in Faith," WSJ.com, June 6, 2008 <http://online.wsj.com/article/SB121271181887250603.html>.

p. 161   every survey suggests that this pattern is becoming more pronounced: See for instance the Pew Forum's "Summary of

Key Findings" on religious affiliation <http://religions.pew forum.org/reports>.

p. 164   mission to a culture that was previously Christian: See Lesslie Newbigin, *The Gospel in a Pluralist Society* (Grand Rapids: Eerdmans, 1989).

Kingdom Focus, Missional Encounters

Churches for the Sake of Others (C4SO) is led by the Rt. Reverend Dr. Todd Hunter. As an initiative of the Anglican Mission in the Americas (AMiA), C4SO is launching a church planting movement designed to develop leaders committed to planting Kingdom-based, missional churches located primarily, but not exclusively, on the West Coast of the United States.

"Todd Hunter is uniquely gifted and equipped for this ministry. His tremendous passion for, and experience with, planting churches shaped around Kingdom-based, missional encounters with contemporary culture is just what we need for our West Coast Initiative."

—THE RT. REV. CHARLES H. MURPHY, III, ANGLICAN MISSION CHAIRMAN